The Smoker Cookbook

Tasty Smoked Meat Recipes to Cook Like a Pitmaster

Jack Wood

© Copyright 2022 - All rights reserved.

The content contained within this book may not be reproduced, duplicated, or transmitted without direct written permission from the author or the publisher.

Under no circumstances will any blame or legal responsibility be held against the publisher, or author, for any damages, reparation, or monetary loss due to the information contained within this book. Either directly or indirectly.

Legal Notice:

This book is copyright protected. This book is only for personal use. You cannot amend, distribute, sell, use, quote, or paraphrase any part, or the content within this book, without the consent of the author or publisher.

Disclaimer Notice:

Please note the information contained within this document is for educational and entertainment purposes only. All effort has been executed to present accurate, up-to-date, and reliable, complete information. No warranties of any kind are declared or implied. Readers acknowledge that the author is not engaging in the rendering of legal, financial, medical, or professional advice. The content within this book has been derived from various sources. Please consult a licensed professional before attempting any techniques outlined in this book.

By reading this document, the reader agrees that under no circumstances is the author responsible for any losses, direct or indirect, which are incurred as a result of the use of the information contained within this document, including, but not limited to, — errors, omissions, or inaccuracies.

Table of Contents

Introduction 1

The Wood Pellet Smoker & Grill 3

   How It Works 5
      Heat control 5
      Wood pellets 6
      How the Heat Distribution Works in Pellet Smoker Grills 7
      The benefit of Wood Pellet Smoker Grill 7
      Smoking vs. Grilling 9

   The Right Pellet 10
      What should a good pellet look like? 11

   Cleaning and Maintenance 13
      1. A brand-new smoker needs to be seasoned before use 13
      2. A smoker will occasionally have to be repaired and repainted. 14
      3. It needs to be cleaned after every use 14
      Cutting Types 15
      Ribs 16
      Tips & Techniques 16
      Pork shoulder 17
      Tips & Techniques 18
      Tenderloins 18
      Tips & Techniques 19
      Beef 20
      Brisket 21
      Tips & Techniques 21

   Seven Tips to Become a Pitmaster 22
      1. Consistent heat 22

- 2. Smoking meat needs patience 22
- 3. Decide whether you want the smoking process to be dry or wet: 23
- 4. Make sure to choose the right meat for you 23
- 5. Using a rub is substantial in any smoking process 23
- 6. Choose the right wood 23
- 7. The importance of brining in the process of smoking: 24

Seven Tips to Start 24
- 1. Soaking Chips of Wood 24
- 2. Set Smoker 24
- 3. Selecting Meat for Smoking 25
- 4. Getting the Meat Ready 25
- 5. Placing meat into the smoker 26
- 6. Basting Meat 26
- 7. Taking Out Meat 26

Texas Pitmaster Brisket Secrets 27

The Correct Way to Cut and Rub Your Brisket 29
- How to Trim a Brisket 30
- Barbecue Brisket Rub 30

The Cooking Process 31
- How to Place the Brisket on Your Smoker 31
- How Long to Cook It 32
- Managing Your Brisket During the Cook 32
- How to Maintain Brisket Moisture 33
- Wrapping Your Brisket 34

Finishing Your Brisket 35
- Slicing It 35
- How to get organized 35

Rubs & Sauces 37

Classic Kansas City BBQ Sauce 38

- Steak Sauce 39
- Bourbon Whiskey Sauce 40
- Texas-Style Brisket Run 41
- Pork Dry Rub 42
- Brown Sugar Rub 43
- Texas Barbeque Rub 44
- Chicken Marinade 45
- Barbeque Sauce 46
- Carolina Gold BBQ Sauce 47
- Teriyaki Sauce 48
- Thai Chili Sauce 49
- Easy Jerk Seasoning 50

Pork 51
- Smoked Baby Back Ribs 52
- Competition Style BBQ Pork Ribs 53
- Smoked Apple BBQ Ribs 54
- Roasted Ham 55
- Smoked Pork Loin 56
- Smoke Pulled Pork 57
- Barbecue Baby Back Ribs 59
- Maple Baby Back Ribs 60
- Smoked Mustard Baby Back Ribs 62
- Grilled Pork Chops 63

Lemon Pepper Pork Tenderloin 65

Chinese BBQ Pork 67

Beef 69

Wholesome Beef Tri-Tip 70

Meat Chuck Short Rib 72

Reverse-Seared Tri-Tip 74

George's Smoked Tri-Tip 75

Pulled Beef 77

La Rochelle Steak 79

Brined Smoked Brisket 80

Cocoa-Rubbed Steak for Two 81

Smoked Rib-Eye Caps 82

Seared Rib-Eye Steaks 83

BBQ Brisket with Coffee Rub 84

Smoked Texas BBQ Brisket 85

Pastrami Short Ribs 86

Poultry 89

Buffalo Chicken Wings 90

Sweet and Sour Chicken 91

Smoked Chicken with Perfect Poultry Rub 93

Chicken Lollipops 94

Asian Wings 95

Lemon Chicken in Foil Packet 97

Sweet and Spicy Chicken 98

Grilled Chicken 99

Crispy and Juicy Chicken 100

Glazed Chicken Thighs 101

Smoked Stuffed Avocado with Shredded Chicken 102

Teriyaki Smoked Drumstick 104

Bacon Candy Chicken Bites 105

Monterey Chicken 106

Smoke-Roasted Chicken Thighs 107

Maple Smoked Sweet and Spicy Wings 108

Herb Roasted Turkey 110

Turkey Legs 112

Turkey Breast 114

Apple Wood-Smoked Whole Turkey 116

BBQ Whole Turkey 117

Lamb 119

Garlic Lamb Cutlets 120

Smoked Lamb Shoulder 121

Smoked Pulled Lamb Sliders 122

Crown Rack of Lamb 123

Lamb's Leg Traditional Steaks 125

Braised Lamb 'n Apricot 126

Greek-Style Roast Leg of Lamb 127

Smoked Rack of Lamb 129
Smoked Lamb Loin 131
Seasoned Lamb Shoulder 133

Conclusion 135

Introduction

A backyard barbecue with loved ones, neighbors, and friends seems a pleasant scene, doesn't it? When you have guests around, having a smoker grill and some grilled and smoked foods is a great idea. For instance, you may provide delicious cuisine and a romantic moment on a summer night.

The introduction of pellet grills might permanently alter how we prepare food. Nowadays, everyone may buy a pellet grill since companies cater to the needs of customers from all walks of life. Cooking is pleasurable and convenient, thanks to modern pellet grills.

The straightforward instructions and ability to remotely check and modify your temps further remove uncertainty.

A wood pellet grill may quickly become one of the most crucial tools you can purchase to help you produce delectable meals with much less work, whether you're an amateur home chef hosting a backyard barbeque or a pitmaster at a barbecue competition.

Smoking was originally described as a type of art. Any enthusiast may easily grasp the fundamentals and advanced skills with persistent work. It's also suggested that once you perfect and advance your smoking knowledge, you won't consider mastering other culinary methods.

You may test hundreds of wonderful recipes with a wood pellet smoker grill! It is up to you to experiment, make improvements, or create your recipes. The process is quick and simple. But by all means, stick with the tried-and-true methods if you want to be safe. These recipes have a reputation for being perfectly palatable and reliable. Your competitive advantage will come from making the right impression the first time and every time while also indulging in delectable food.

These recipes' ease of preparation and lack of prerequisite culinary expertise make them another amazing item. You can use these recipes to make delicious dishes in no time by having the right ingredients and following a few simple steps.

To spread the word, try these recipes! This recipe book for a wood pellet smoker-grill will undoubtedly be a priceless present for your loved ones!

You no longer need to search the internet for your preferred wood pellet smoker-grill recipes. This book is an all-in-one resource to end your search for the ideal wood pellet smoker-grill recipes for you and your loved ones.

The Wood Pellet Smoker & Grill

JACK WOOD

How It Works

The wood pellet grill is powered by electricity. The hopper is filled with a certain amount of wood pellets descend via a spinning auger.

The needed temperature, specified by a control panel, determines how quickly or gradually the revolving auger feeds the required number of pellet grains into the fire section. A red-hot rod will ignite the pellets after they have been placed in the fire pot, igniting the flames. Then, a fan maintains a mild airflow over the fire area, creating a convection oven-type heat that evenly and gently cooks your food. Above the fire pot is a drip tray that keeps you away from any direct flame action. Additionally, each following leak is caught in this tray to avoid unintended flare-ups.

Indirect grilling is a technique that is often utilized with vintage charcoal and wood smokers. Many early users switched to wood pellet grills due to this similarity and how wood pellets impart smoky tastes to meals. It is a simple substitute for conventional smokers. Some pellet grill makers have Wi-Fi controls built, allowing you to monitor the grill from a distance.

The design techniques used to create wood pellet smoker grills are not new. However, the grills are definitely creating a buzz in the grill marketplaces. People want to know whether using these grills is safe. Yes, food-grade wood pellets are no riskier to prepare food with than any other option.

Heat control

The amount of energy the burning fire uses and the steadiness of the airflow both have a significant role in how much heat the wood pellet grill produces. In contrast to other grills, smoker grills operate with automated air and fire supply, which helps to control steady heat.

The automatic heat system's desired heat setting is configured to accomplish this. The firepot is then supplied with some pellets by a motorized auger. Depending on the grill manufacturer, the igniter rod ignites the wood pellets and modifies the fire rate to raise the grill heat to an opening temperature of 60° to 82° Celsius. The preferred temperature is accomplished by repeating the duty cycle when the fire is ready. One duty cycle begins when the rotating auger starts to feed the pellets into the firepot and later continues when it becomes off and is in sleep mode.

When the auger turns back on, the duty period is over. For example, a wood pellet grill set to 122 °C may have an active phase lasting 12 seconds, followed by a 40-second rest phase. A duty phase is a time when the auger is operational. The auger will perform a full-duty revolution once it is turned on. The auger is only ON for 50% of that time and is given a 50% duty succession. Each heat temperature results in a different duty cycle. The active auger duration remains constant regardless of the amount of heat applied. The only time that changes is the auger-off period.

Wood pellets

Some pellets used for general heating may include softwood and other wood scraps (wood bark), giving food an unpleasant flavor or taste and perhaps being poisonous if consumed. On the other hand, pellet grills use food-grade wood pellets to fuel them. They are constructed of compressed wood dust and measure one inch in length and one-quarter inch in breadth. The wood dust remains placed under high heat and pressure. As a result, the chemical lignin, a plant-based glue that exists naturally in wood, is stimulated. The only additives in the wood pellets are the vegetable oils that are added to aid in adherence and enhance the taste. The pellet burns thoroughly and leaves little to no ash behind. Mesquite, maple, oak, alder, cherry, hickory, apple, and pecan are a few of the wood pellet varieties produced.

How the Heat Distribution Works in Pellet Smoker Grills

The firebox's heat shield helps to transmit heat evenly to the grill's two sides. As a result, air rises and enters the chamber of the convection grill. Then, at a remarkable pace of 10 times per second, a sensor inside the grill transmits data electronically to the onboard computer. The controller then modifies the airflow and pellet distribution system to maintain the desired temperature.

The benefit of Wood Pellet Smoker Grill

Using a pellet barbecue to cook is a novel and distinctive experience. Hardwood pellets give the meat product a genuine woodsy, smokey taste. You can rely on the new pellet smoker grills to do the task independently. The user configures them to operate automatically.

The main and most noticeable distinction is that a pellet grill makes it far comfier to manage temperatures and unwind since it offers the user an automatic air and fuel delivery system.

Think again if you believe that controlling the cooking temperature in a smoker is just too difficult. Pellet grills are essentially a "set it and forget it" method of grilling since they eliminate the trouble and anxiety that conventional smokers demand.

As if that weren't enough, pellet grills provide you with even more. You now have the utmost ease of mixing a variety of cooking alternatives with your new pellet grill. Old-fashioned smokers only smoke food, so if you want to grill, bake, or roast food, you need to buy different units for each activity.

In contrast to gas or propane barbecues, pellet grills give greater control. Both gas barbecues and pellet grills provide the outdoor cook with a unique set of useful features. Even still, if they looked more attentively, you would see some noticeable variations. Gas grills are ideal for culinary tasks, but their inadequate insulation often do not function well at low cooking temperatures. It's important to set up older models of propane grills so that they get the right amount of airflow. This, alone, makes them a poor choice for smokers. The Pellet Grill is a no-brainer in today's world!

With pellet grills, the cook has access to additional taste combinations. The wood pellets used in pellet grills come in various tastes. Thanks to this, you may use your pellet smoker grill to cook all of the items. Sure, they both cook your food, but the pellet grill is far superior in many aspects. The Pellet Smoker Grill is the only option for me!

After that, you must decide whether to use a pellet grill or stick with the popular charcoal grilling technique.

For a very long time, charcoal grills have been regarded as the absolute best for outdoor cooking. There are various layout options for charcoal grills, but only two fuel options: lump charcoal or charcoal briquettes. Charcoal grilling is unquestionably a labor of love. It's okay that some individuals I know will go to great lengths to protect them. We are all unique, and that is a positive thing as well. However, using a charcoal barbecue for cooking is not that simple. To make all the components perfect, much experience is required, and temperature management is challenging.

Pellet grills may be used for grilling and smoking, making the process much simpler. They have become the top seller in the country for this reason. Even in terms of cleanliness, there is no comparison between the two methods. With the pellet grill, you will have no problems. It will be very easy to clean it every time you use it. Classic grills, on the other hand, require a lot of work, and in some cases, you really need to throw them away and buy new ones.

A comparison between the established Electric Smoker, which is widely accessible in the backyard cooking market, and the pellet smoker grills would be another thing to consider. Today's electric smokers are actually modern takes on classic smokers and offer lots of control. To get optimal results, electric smokers heat wood chips. They are quite convenient to operate and allow the chef in your family to set it and forget it. When you have to grill and sear, the issue emerges. For that, you require very high temperatures, often between 450 and 550 degrees. The good news is that electric smokers can reach temperatures high enough for most culinary tasks.

Smoking vs. Grilling

The cooking temperature of the meal is the primary distinction between smokers and grills. A grill cooks food at 300 degrees F or more, whereas a smoker cooks it at a lower temperature (about 225 degrees F). This is crucial because grill metal has to be more resilient than grill metal, which uses high heat when food is grilled at a lower temperature. A grill's high heat can burn most cooking oil left in the fire chamber, but a smoker's lower heat can't accomplish that, thus the fat is left behind.

The Right Pellet

A wood pellet smoker and grill is special because it uses wood pellets as fuel. Compressed sawdust from pine, birch, fir, or plant stalks makes wood pellets. Wood pellets are mostly utilized as fuel for pellet smokers and grills in the culinary world. They may also be used for home heating, however. But the taste variety of wood pellets for cooking makes them unique. Speaking of tastes, here is a brief overview of the flavors of wood pellets for you:

- Apple & Cherry Pellets: The taste of these pellets is moderate, sweet, and smokey. They may improve mild meat, often the preferred taste when preparing pork or poultry. These pellets are quite delicate, despite their ability to generate excellent smoke.

- Alder Pellets: This particular pellet has a hint of sweetness but is otherwise moderate and neutral. This flavor is the one to choose if you want a substantial quantity of smoke without overpowering delicate meats like fish and poultry.

- Hickory Pellets: Hickory pellets provide a savory, smoky, and bacon-like taste. These pellets are the ones that are often used for grilling. This pellet may sometimes be too thick and smoky and become overbearing. If so, think about combining it with apple or oak pellets.

- Maple Pellets: Maple pellets are the greatest choice if you're seeking something moderate with a touch of sweetness. They are excellent for pork or poultry.

- Mesquite Pellets: Mesquite pellets are a preferred alternative for Texas barbecue because of their strong, spicily, and tangy taste.

- Oak Pellets: In between apple and hickory are oak pellets. They are a great option for cooking fish or vegetables since they are slightly milder than the latter and a bit stronger than the former.

- Pecan Pellets: A perennial favorite is pecan. Hickory-like in taste, yet with a hint of vanilla and nutty undertones. Pecan pellets are incredibly appealing and suitable for all of them, making them the ideal pellets for beef and chicken.

What should a good pellet look like?

With the hundreds of various wood pellet variations and brands, it might be challenging to decide which brand to take into consideration. Try at least the top three brands you are familiar with and evaluate their performance if you are unsure about the brand to choose.

- **Appearance:** When selecting a wood pellet brand, the look of the pellets should come first. Once you've used wood pellets for a while, you'll be able to determine and assess their quality based just on appearance. The length of the pellets should be examined first. Brands follow established guidelines, so this aspect is not important. However, you must be aware that when it comes to pellet fuels, length factors into the performance of the pellets. Another thing to consider is the dust you will discover in the package. Once the bag is opened, it is common to notice fines; however, if there are an unusually high fines, the pellets are likely of poor quality.

- **Texture:** Another factor is the pellets' texture. There is a distinct texture to wood pellets. The pellets are high-quality if they feel smooth and glossy to the touch. The same holds if there are no breaks in the pellets. Pellets are poor if they have excessive surface roughness or strange surface racks. Incorrect pressing ratios and high moisture levels in the raw materials used to make the pellets are often to blame.

- **Smell:** Wood pellets are made by exposing them to high temperatures within a sealed space. The lignin in the biomass material gets combined with other substances throughout the process, giving off the aroma of freshly burned wood. There is a good risk that the pellets have not been properly treated or include impure raw materials if they smell terrible.

A further technique to evaluate the quality of wood pellets is to observe how they respond to water and their look, texture, and fragrance. Several minutes should pass while a handful of pellets are allowed to settle in a water basin. The quality of the pellets may be determined by how rapidly they dissolve and expand in water. On the other hand, the pellets are of poor quality if they do not disintegrate after a few minutes but instead expand and become rigid.

Try burning some of the pellets as well, as a final step. The flame produced by high-quality wood pellets will be brilliant and brown. On the other hand, if the flame they produce is black, the pellets are of poor quality. Additionally, high-quality pellets create a small amount of ash; if the pellets leave you with many leftovers, the pellets are poor quality.

Wood to Meat Pairing Chart

Flavor	Beef	Pork	Seafood	Lamb	Game Meat
Apple	X	X	X		
Alder		X		X	
Hickory	X	X		X	X
Mesquite	X	X	X		
Oak		X		X	X
Pecan	X	X		X	X

Cleaning and Maintenance

The tools, including a grill smoker, must be maintained, especially if you want to smoke often and your gear to endure. Three guidelines for using a smoker:

1. A brand-new smoker needs to be seasoned before use

Cooking oil or bacon grease must first be applied to the inside surface of the smoker to season it.

When heated, the oil will permeate every pore in the smoker's metal surface. By doing this, a rust-preventing barrier will be created.

The smoker has to be heated to a temperature of between 250–275 degrees Fahrenheit. Avoid exceeding this temperature since doing so might harm the paint. You can use charcoal, but it's better to use the sort of fuel you plan to use for smoking food. For two or three hours, keep the smoker at this temperature.

Even though the instruction manual does not specifically state that seasoning is necessary, it is still preferable to turn on your smoker than not since it eliminates all the chemicals used in the production process. You can then be certain that your food is toxin-free.

2. A smoker will occasionally have to be repaired and repainted

Your smoker will sometimes need to be cleaned, even if you don't use it often. Cleaning it with a wire brush and sandpaper may remove all of the rust. Clean it completely, then repaint it using BBQ paint that is heat resistant. If you take proper care of it, a high-quality smoker may endure for decades, if not a lifetime. Remember that your smoker's condition impacts the flavor of the food you make in it. Consequently, regular maintenance is crucial.

3. It needs to be cleaned after every use

To take good care of your smoker, you must regularly remove the ash and prevent food buildup. However, although a smoker requires occasional scrubbing, the protective coating must not be damaged, so you should never scrub the smoker down to the bare metal.

You may need to regularly wipe it out and season it if you've owned it for a while or use it often. You must keep the metal's smoky, greasy surface in good condition to avoid rusting.

After usage, ash should never be left in the smoker since it might collect water and cause rusting. It is necessary to carefully scrape away large grease deposits that have been stuck to the metal. A well-maintained smoker not only lives longer but also improves the flavor of your meal.

Cutting Types

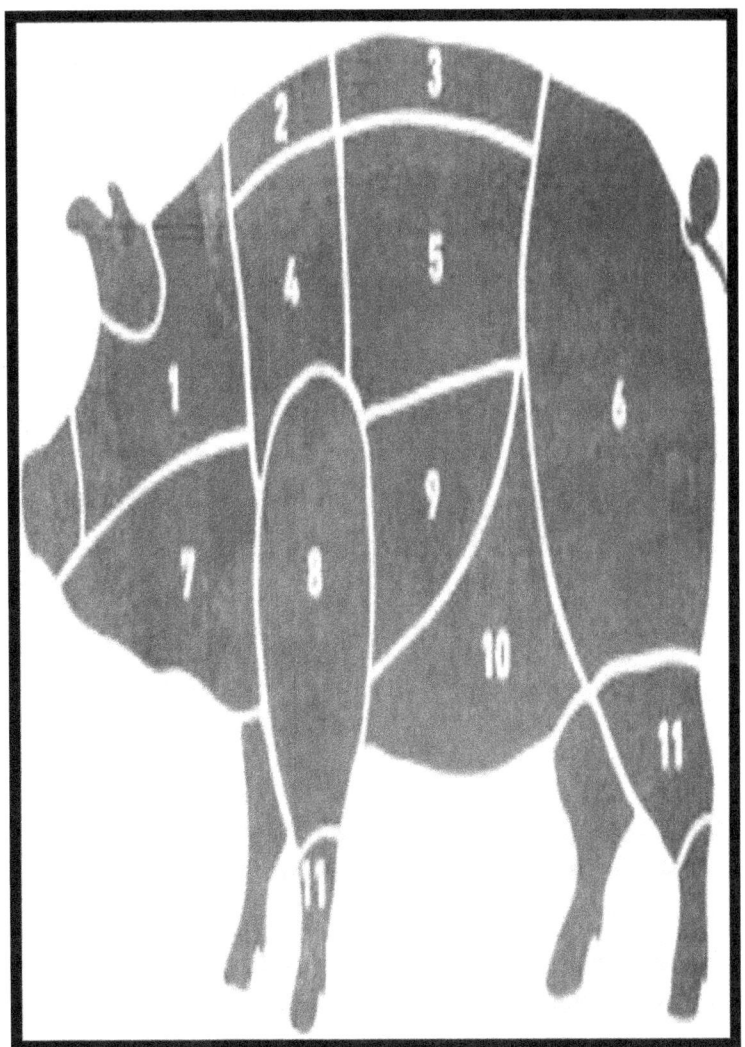

Pork

1. Head
2. Clear Plate
3. Back Fat
4. Boston Butt/Shoulder
5. Loin/ Tenderloin
6. Ham
7. Cheek
8. Picnic Shoulder
9. Ribs
10. Bacon/Belly
11. Hock

Although pork may not be my preferred meat, it could be my finest. I've prepared ribs and hog shoulders for my barbecue for hours. Pork was a fantastic place to start since I often host big gatherings, including an annual game of Bad Santa with my rowdy high school pals.

There is no mistaking the taste of salt in pork. Although it sometimes gets in the way, the fat content in pork makes meat juicy and tender.

I often mention how wonderfully pork pairs with sweet tastes. Purchase some local honey to help the local beekeepers, farmers, and markets. Local honey also has a greater flavor. Additionally, wonderful with pork is brown sugar. And every time I visit a friend in Toronto, I always stop at the duty-free store on the way home to get some Canadian maple syrup to have on hand for dishes with pork.

Ribs

I'll use broad phrases when discussing pork ribs, spare ribs, and baby backs. In both situations, you should choose a cut with a considerable amount of fat, but it should be evenly distributed. Too much fat, especially if it is only in certain places, can make for an unappetizingly fatty bite.

Our ribs will be prepared differently than they would be in a chain barbecue restaurant in your community. These will have the slightest pull to them before the meat slips and falls off the bone. Cook them a bit longer if you want the flesh to fall off the bone.

Tips & Techniques

Take the membrane off. Ribs may become less delicate and tougher to peel off the bone because of that strange membrane on the back of the ribs (also known as silver skin). Remove the membrane to consistently produce outcomes at the pitmaster level.

Apply mustard as glue. Mustard performs well when used as a binder for your rub on fatty foods like ribs. Before or after your rub, spread some simple yellow or smooth mustard over your ribs. This will keep your rub on your meat and not all over your drip pan.

For your spritz or your wrap, use any drink you like (including beer or wine, but avoid liquor). I questioned why when I saw a contestant chef prepare ribs with Mountain Dew. He said, "My brother and I just started using it because that's what we like and have.". I use Pepsi; my dad and brother use apple juice. Use what you like, see what other pitmasters are using and try that for a change. It's a great place to experiment.

Sauce it—just don't overdo it. Again, saucing is a real preference. I usually serve a dish of dry-rubbed ribs during parties. My ribs have gone from being dry to being extensively sauced throughout the years, and now I simply use a thin sweet coating. We also have various methods to achieve sweetness, as you can see in the recipes.

Pork shoulder

Pitmasters are huge fans of pulled pork. Not only is it convenient and practical, but it also usually results in days' worth of leftovers. Sliders, nachos, and sandwiches are all variations of pulled-pork leftover week foods served in the next two or three days. A good-size pork shoulder could feed an army—or at least an army of kids just back from baseball, gymnastics, or soccer.

It is irrelevant whether you pick a pork shoulder with or without a bone when choosing your pork shoulder, commonly known as pork butt or Boston butt. Some individuals will claim that it does, but it depends on the individual. Check the fat content, however. Pork needs some fat to prevent drying out, but too much may become too fatty, similar to ribs. The fat cap should be less than 1 inch deep.

Tips & Techniques

Pork shoulder may be injected for more taste and moisture. Inject your shoulder with tea. While a right shoulder's bark will be pleasant and tasty, injecting it will make it taste everywhere. For a nice "bark," smoke your meat longer. The bark is that delicious crust on the outside of well-smoked meat. The bark forms when the meat and rub are continuously smoked for a long time. A nice, black bark is a sign of a quality pork shoulder. Smoke the pork longer, uncovered, to produce more bark.

Pull the meat using your hands; it's simply simpler. Some brand-new, amusing claws can be used to pull pork. Your hands don't become warm and greasy from them. However, the pull with them never quite seems right. I have an inexpensive pair of cotton gloves under food service gloves. The gloves allow me to pull the meat precisely as I want it while preventing my hands from burning.

Tenderloins

Even though they need one of the easiest smoke grilling techniques, pork tenderloins are always spectacular. Every few weeks, I grill a few tenderloins for my family, and they never grow tired of them. Tenderloins cook well on the pellet grill or smoker, producing consistently juicy results.

Fat content is important in choosing tenderloins, like with most pork. I make an effort to keep my tenderloins' fat level low. A pellet grill will work to keep them moist and will define dried-out areas.

Tips & Techniques

To save time, just smoke them. The pellet grill's Smoke setting does a superb job of bringing your meat to temperature while always keeping it moist.

Reverse the sear. Typically, the meat is seared before being fully cooked. We refer to it as a reverse sear when we finish the process after the meat has completely smoked. Use your grill's open flame option, such as the flame broiler, if it has one; if not, raise the temperature as high as it will go. The tenderloins should be smoked until they reach an internal temperature of 135°F to 140°F. Then, sear them on each side for 3 to 5 minutes at a higher temperature until they reach 145°F.

Pork tenderloins make a fantastic marinade candidate. Pork tenderloin marinated in teriyaki sauce has a delicious flavor and may absorb the marinade's flavor in as little as 30 minutes.

Beef

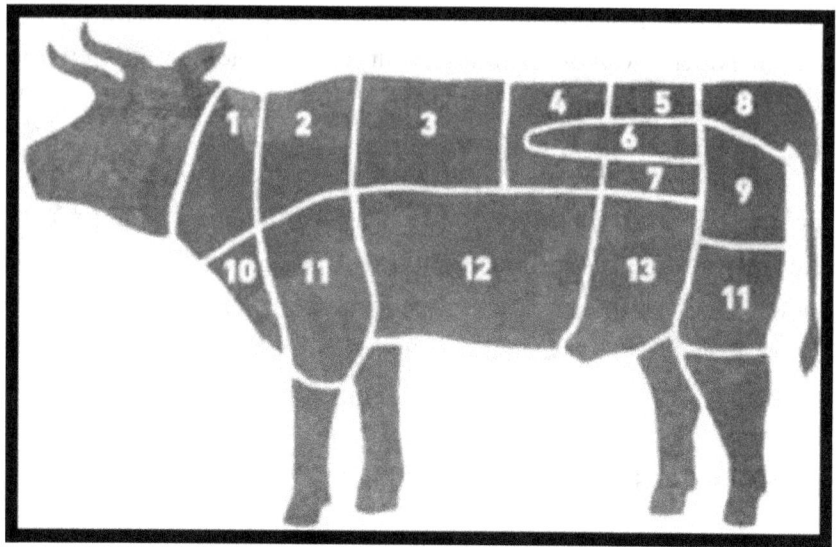

1. Neck
2. Chuck
3. Rib
4. Short Loin
5. Sirloin
6. Tenderloin
7. Top Sirloin
8. Rump Cap
9. Round
10. Brisket
11. Shoulder Clod
12. Short Plate
13. Flank

When I think of smoking and barbecue, I instantly think of beef: large tri-tip and brisket slices, flame-grilled steaks. Fortunately, all of these can be prepared on a pellet barbecue thanks to modern grill technology.

But the ideal Texas-style brisket is what so many pitmasters strive for. We've all devoted hours to finding the most effective methods to do it: Is it wrapped or not? Butcher paper or foil? How long ought it to last? Additionally, we want steaks that even the greatest steakhouse proprietor would pay for— steaks with the aroma of seared meat permeating the smoke, butter, and fire. We strive to achieve that in our backyards.

Due to this, whenever I think of smoking or grilling, I think of "beef." The quality of beef makes choosing it simpler. We'll go into this here and some other tips to make you a master of low-and-slow meat cooking.

Brisket

Brisket is often the best and trickiest meat to cook on a pellet grill, in my experience. Many people reverently observe the ideal brisket in the hopes that one day they will succeed in making one. Discussions on the bend, pull, and similar tests are common on message boards. What is wrong with this way of thinking about brisket? Actually, making it isn't that tough. Like everything else, brisket can be mastered with time and effort.

When selecting the perfect brisket—with both the point and flat cuts (usually separated at most butchers) intact—the key is not too much fat. If you get a brisket with an enormous fat cap, you will just chop it off. Additionally, I advise investing the additional cash in the best brisket you can find. A cheap brisket can equal a tough brisket. Spend the money on the finest cut, as brisket is not a cheap cut in the first place.

Tips & Techniques

Remove that fat cap. The meat won't be as tasty if you smoke your brisket without removing the huge fat cap. Cut the fat cap to around 1/4 inch with a boning knife or other appropriate tool. Your brisket's fattiness may be reduced by trimming the fat cap, but keeping it partly on will keep the meat juicy.

Wrap. Never wrap. Your decision. Both aluminum foil and butcher paper can be used for wrapping—again, it is all about preference. However, the one thing I recommend regarding wrapping is to wait until 165°F to 170°F after the stall. If you wrap your meat too soon, your bark won't grow as much, and your brisket won't be as smokey.

Use a water pan or spray the meat if you don't want to wrap it. Your brisket will remain moist if you spritz it with liquid like apple juice or simple water. Like any other form of barbecue, a water pan may be used with a pellet grill, but be cautious not to spill it. Simply insert a metal pan inside the grill, filled with water. The water pan will fit well if you have a flat drain pan.

Seven Tips to Become a Pitmaster

Every chef in the world has as their goal to master the art of smoking food. Each of us must adhere to certain fundamentals and guidelines to develop the art of smoking food.

So, now that you're prepared to start light your smoker, begin. Here are some suggestions to help you experience the flavor you want:

1. Consistent heat

Smoking food needs a low heat and keeps it quiet for a few hours allowing the smoke to penetrate through the meats. Keeping the heat steady is crucial to enhance your smoking experience. This procedure may be rather simple. To heat your coals to a temperature of roughly 250° F, use a chimney starter. Holding your palm over the coals is the easiest technique to check the temperature if you don't have a thermometer.

It is simple; all you have to do is to pile the coals over the bottom, add the smoking wood, and put the meat onto the grill right into the opposite side of the coals you use. If you want to keep the temperature the same, you may always add coals occasionally.

2. Smoking meat needs patience

Meat smoking is a time-consuming procedure that takes many hours. For instance, slowly smoking meat results in soft morsels of meat that retain their taste and juiciness.

There are several kinds of meat. It takes each variety between 5 and 7 hours to smoke it correctly. When smoking, avoid peeking at your food unless you need to add additional coals to keep the temperature regulated or top up the water pan.

3. Decide whether you want the smoking process to be dry or wet:

The wet smoking method uses a pan with water and charcoal to moisten the meat by producing a smoky environment. You can also use fruit juice or any other types of equipment that have to add extra flavors. People will like the delicious bark produced by wet smoking.

4. Make sure to choose the right meat for you

Not all meats can be smoked; chicken and turkey are decent options, but the skin won't hold up since the smoking process takes a long time. Besides, brining will help you through the process of smoking.

5. Using a rub is substantial in any smoking process

Making the rub before smoking food is crucial. You may mix around 1/2 cup of kosher salt with 2 teaspoons of chili flakes, 1 tablespoon of lemon pepper, 1/2 cup of brown sugar, and 1 tablespoon of black pepper to make the ideal rub. Just before smoking, rub the meat with this mixture.

6. Choose the right wood

You should carefully choose the wood you will use to smoke meat. For example, using apple wood will give you a sweet and fruity smoke that pairs well with pork, while hickory wood is a terrific option for red meat like ribs. Alder meat goes well with fish, chicken, and other white meat.

Pecan wood burns more coolly than other types of wood, making it an ideal option for roasts of pork and brisket. Depending on the sort of meat and taste you want, you may also use cherry and oak wood and other foods.

7. The importance of brining in the process of smoking:

Brining any meat helps prevent it from drying out while it is smoked. The proteins may become more water-absorbent due to the salt in the brine. Indeed, the sodium and the chloride ions get into the protein tissue to hold onto the moisture. Marinating the meat in the brine for 10–12 hours before smoking it is advised.

Seven Tips to Start

1. Soaking Chips of Wood

They must soak to make wood chips last longer as a fuel source for smoking. The reason is dry wood that burns quickly adds fuel to the smoker, resulting in dry smoked meat. When smoking for a shorter time, there is no need to utilize wood chips. Before smoking, prepare the wood chips by soaking them in water for at least 4 hours. Then drain the chips, cover them in aluminum foil, and seal them. Make holes in the bag of wood chips with a toothpick or fork.

2. Set Smoker

Each sort of smoker uniquely develops their habit. For smokers using wood or charcoal, ignite half of the briquettes and wait until they lose their flame. Then, if using, add the remaining charcoal and wood chips. Wait until they are fully lit and emitting heat before pushing the charcoal away and positioning the meat on the other side of the cooking grate. Indirect smoking of the meat over low heat is ensured by doing this. Continue filling the smoker with charcoal and/or moistened wood chips.

For a gas/propane or electric smoker, just switch it on following the manufacturer's instructions, add soaked wood chips to the chip holder, and fill the water container, if one is provided, with water. To keep track of the smoker's interior temperature, either utilize the built-in thermostat or purchase a separate one. Add meat to the smoker after it has reached the proper preheated temperature.

3. Selecting Meat for Smoking

Choose the type of meat that tastes good with a smoky flavor. Following meat goes well for smoking.

Beef: ribs, brisket and corned beef.

Pork: spare ribs, roast, shoulder, and ham.

Poultry: whole chicken, whole turkey, and big game hens. Seafood: Salmon, scallops, trout, and lobster.

4. Getting the Meat Ready

Cook the meat as directed per the recipe. Occasionally, meat is merely seasoned with the rub, marinated or both. Using these techniques, smoked meat is guaranteed to be tasty, tender, and juicy.

Brine is a treatment option for ham, hog, or poultry. It includes adding meat after the brine components have been dissolved in a large water container. After letting it soak for at least 8 hours, thoroughly rinse it and pat it dry before you start smoking.

Treat beef or briskets with a marinade to enhance the taste. It's better to make deep cuts in meat to let marinate ingredients deep into it. Meat should be drained or smoked right immediately.

Rubs are often used on meat, chicken, or ribs. They are essentially a mixture of salt and a variety of spices that are liberally applied to the meat. The meat is then allowed to rest for at least two hours or more before being smoked.

Make sure the meat is at room temperature before smoking it. As a result, the meat will be cooked consistently and will finish the smoking process at the proper internal temperature.

5. Placing meat into the smoker

Don't place the meat directly overheat into the smoker because the primary purpose of smoking is cooking meat at low temperatures. Place the meat on one side of the smoker, your fuel on the other, and let the meat cook.

Meat's interior temperature determines how long it needs to smoke. Use a meat thermometer for this and place it in the area of the thickest meat. The size of the meat also affects how long it takes to smoke. See recipes to find the precise time to smoke the meat.

6. Basting Meat

The meat is brushed with thin solution, sauces, or marinades in several recipes. This procedure enhances the flavor of the meat while also assisting in preserving moisture throughout the smoking phase. To determine if basting is required, read the recipe.

7. Taking Out Meat

Remove the meat from the smoker after it reaches the correct internal temperature. Normally, when the internal temperature of the fowl hits 165 degrees F, it should be taken out of the smoker. The internal temperature of ground beef, ham, and pork should be 160 degrees Fahrenheit. The internal temperature of chops, roasts, and steaks is 145 degrees Fahrenheit.

Texas Pitmaster Brisket Secrets

JACK WOOD

Brisket is a famously challenging beef cut to master. A brisket has been transformed into a chunk of beef jerky by many inexperienced pitmasters. But don't be deterred by these terrifying tales. After a long 12-hour wait on your smoker, there is no better result than slicing a juicy, perfectly cooked brisket.

In this guide, we walk you through every step of the procedure, from selecting the brisket to trimming, cooking, and controlling the fire.

Whether you've smoked brisket before or this is your first time, there is a ton of excellent tips available.

The Correct Way to Cut and Rub Your Brisket

The main drawback of brisket is that it is a tough cut of beef. This makes it ideal for cooking on low and slow. No special rubs, mops, marinades, or BBQ sauce will make great brisket.

Before you even light up your smoker, choosing the ideal brisket from the butcher shop and correctly preparing it will lead you to success.

We advise asking your local butcher or visiting stores like Costco or Sams Club to get brisket.

Snake River Farms sells premium American Wagyu brisket and ships it anywhere in the contiguous United States if you want to have something special.

In order to have complete control over the cutting procedure, we advise purchasing a whole packer brisket. To make sure that the leaner part cooks at the same rate as the fatter part, try to buy a marbled meat and a thick dish.

Also, look for Certified Angus Beef, USDA Choice, or Prime Beef.

How to Trim a Brisket

Knowing how to cut your brisket will get you very close to your ultimate goal. Here are some important tips:

- To trim the brisket, use a good narrow, curved boning knife.

- If you do not trim the fat, you risk getting an overly fatty flavor, while you risk getting dry meat if you trim too much. Try to get around 1/4" of fat.

- Trimming the brisket while it is still cold will be much easier. To prevent the thinner pieces from cooking too quickly and eventually burning, remove them

- The deckle, which is very thick, will not render out during cooking, so remove it.

- Consider where the heat will come from and how you'll position the brisket on your cooking surface. A little more fat can help protect the meat in hotter areas.

- Trimming isn't as important as getting a decent form and leaving approximately 1/4" of fat on. Practice makes perfect.

Barbecue Brisket Rub

The only ingredients allowed in a proper Texas-style brisket rub are equal parts salt and black pepper. This simple method will give you a fantastic bark without affecting the flavor of the meat too much.

Instead, most pitmasters prefer to include a few more. On their brisket, they use complex rubs with paprika, cumin, and chili powder. You may still refer to it as a Texas brisket by adding a little paprika and garlic spice.

Applying excessive amounts of rub is the biggest error people make. To make the taste of the meat stand out, you want to use a minimal amount of rub.

As you apply the mixture, be sure to swirl it because the salt may sink to the bottom.

Using your hand to catch rub, and put it back on, rub the edges of the brisket. For a more even cook, allow the brisket to come to room temperature for an hour before placing it on the smoker.

The night before you intend to cook your brisket is the best time to trim it. In this manner, you can rub salt into the area and give it plenty of time to soak in. The additional benefit of doing this is that everything is already prepared, allowing you to concentrate on starting your smoker promptly.

The Cooking Process

The techniques for preparing, smoking, and cutting brisket can be used whether you use a grill, a charcoal smoker, a pellet grill, or an offset smoker.

How to Place the Brisket on Your Smoker

A doubt that many people have is whether to place the fat side upward or downward. It's debatable how much of a difference this really makes, but the correct method relies on how your smoker is set up. We recommend placing the brisket fat side up.

Depending on your smoker, you might want to consider smoking fat-side down to prevent the muscle from too drying out if the heat is coming from below.

Bring the brisket's fattier part closer to the flames. The additional fat will aid in insulating it.

The brisket's flat end ought to be closer to the smoke stack. To preserve moisture in the cooking chamber and prevent burning, always use a water pan.

How Long to Cook It

A seasoned pitmaster will tritely respond that you should cook a brisket until it is tender if you ask him how long to cook one.

Based on a variety of variables, two briskets of comparable size may cook at very different rates.

But how can we get an estimate of how long our brisket will need to smoke? 1 hour and 15 minutes per LB (0.45 kg) of brisket at 250°F (120°C) is a decent rule of thumb for estimating how long a brisket will take to cook.

For example: 5lb Brisket x 1.25 hours = 6 hours and 15 minutes cooked at 250°F.

Managing Your Brisket During the Cook

Some important tips:

- When cooking your brisket, always keep an eye on the smoker, trying to keep the temperature constant.
- Do not always open the lid to check; otherwise, you will lose heat and smoke, and it will not be easy to recover them. You can use a wireless dual probe thermometer so

that you can measure the temperature of the smoker and the temperature inside the meat.

- A spray bottle with apple juice or apple cider vinegar is a great remedy if you feel like the meat is drying out too much.

- Try to prevent completely cutting off the oxygen, as this can start a "dirty fire." As a result, creosote, a thick, oily by product of fire, may be produced, giving the food a harsh, over smoked flavor.

- Avoid using green or too cured wood when choosing the wood for your brisket. An excellent solution is Post Oak, a wood seasoned for 9-12 months.

- You want to see clear heat and little smoke emanating from the smoker.

- Try to keep an even temperature, but don't panic if you don't get it perfect on your first brisket. Knowing your cooker and how to regulate your fire only comes from a lot of practice.

How to Maintain Brisket Moisture

The easiest approach to keep moisture in the brisket is to keep a water pan in the smoker. After the first two to three hours, begin spraying the brisket every half-hour to an hour with water, apple juice, spicy sauce, or apple cider vinegar. This keeps it wet and prevents burning.

Some people soak the meat with a liquid combination, but this makes a big mess and may damage the brisket's bark.

Wrapping Your Brisket

Wrapping the brisket in aluminum foil (the Texas crutch) or butcher paper is an optional step that can be useful in some circumstances.

For example, if your smoker emits too much smoke, wrapping the meat could be a solution. In addition, wrapping is useful for speeding up cooking time, helping to retain moisture and get through the stall faster.

But what is a stall? The internal temperature rises quickly at first when cooking a sizable piece of meat at low temperatures, such as brisket. The moisture that is inside the meat starts to escape from the center and evaporates on the center as the meat cooks.

You have two choices when the stall happens: you can wrap your meat or you can ride it out.

You can go through the stall by wrapping it since it keeps the moisture inside the foil or butcher paper.

In other words, braising your meat causes the internal temperature to increase more quickly and results in a dish that is incredibly juicy and tender.

When to wrap it? On the best time to wrap beef, barbecue gurus disagree strongly. I think it's a good idea to wrap your brisket if either of the following has occurred:

1. When stalling occurs or when the internal temperature has reached 165°F (whichever comes first).
2. After a dark bark has formed

Usually, these two cases occur after about 4 hours, more or less, depending on the smoking temperature and other variables.

Finishing Your Brisket

You might wish to wrap your brisket when it has a good bark formed but is still supple and malleable.

Once wrapped, return the brisket to 250°F until cooked through, that is, when the internal temperature reaches 195°-203°F. With experience, you will learn to recognize the right cooking point just by looking at and touching your brisket.

Slicing It

Let the brisket rest 1 hour after you take it out of the cooker before beginning to slice it.

Cutting a brisket properly involves cutting across the grain on the flat side until you reach the point. After which, cut against the grain after rotating the brisket 90 degrees.

Use a 12" serrated knife and try to avoid scraping the bark. On the fattiest portion, slice each piece to the thickness of a large pencil, and on the leanest, to the thickness of a tiny pencil.

Leave the brisket whole if you won't be using it right away, and trim it soon before serving to prevent drying out. A cooler should be used to store the cooked brisket for a few hours. Make sure it is wrapped in butcher paper, foil, and, finally a towel.

Brisket is a severely unbalanced beef cut. There are fatty, lean, thick, and thin regions in every piece. This explains why mastering it can take so long.

How to get organized

It is very difficult for you to be ready at the exact time you want to serve dinner.

The best course of action is to try to prepare it at least an hour beforehand. Wrap the brisket in foil and an old towel once it reaches a temperature of around 203°F, and then put it in a beer cooler.

An excellent technique is the faux cambro technique which will allow you to store the meat for up to 3 hours:

1. Pour some hot water into the cooler before the meat is done and shut the lid to let the water heat up.

2. Remove the water and line the container with some old towels to insulate it in case of leakage.

Rubs & Sauces

Classic Kansas City BBQ Sauce

Preparation time: 10 Minutes
Cooking time: 15 Minutes
Servings: 24

INGREDIENTS:

- 1/4 cup yellow onion, finely chopped
- 2 tablespoons water
- 2 tablespoons vegetable oil
- 2 cups ketchup
- 1/3 cup brown sugar
- 3 cloves garlic, finely chopped
- 1 tablespoon apple cider vinegar
- 1 tablespoon tomato paste
- 1 tablespoon Worcestershire sauce
- 1 teaspoon liquid hickory smoke
- 1 teaspoon ground mustard

DIRECTIONS:

1. The onion should be placed in a food processor and pulse until smooth. The onion will be pulsed once more after the addition of the water.
2. Heat the oil in a medium skillet, then add the onion. Add the additional ingredients and mix well when the onion is just beginning to soften.
3. The sauce has to boil for 15 minutes while being stirred periodically.
4. Before using the pan or putting it in a mason jar, remove the pan from the heat and allow it to cool for 30 minutes.

NUTRITION: Calories: 799, Sodium: 595mg, Dietary Fiber: 8.6g, Fat: 52.7g, Carbs: 74.9g, Protein: 10g

Steak Sauce

Preparation time: 5 Minutes
Cooking time: 20 Minutes
Servings: 1/2 Cup

INGREDIENTS:

- 1 Tbsp. Malt vinegar
- 1/2 Tsp. Salt
- 1/2 Tsp. black pepper
- 1 Tbsp. Tomato sauce
- 2 Tbsp. brown sugar
- 1 Tsp. hot pepper sauce
- 2 Tbsp. Worcestershire sauce
- 2 Tbsp. Raspberry jam.

DIRECTIONS:

1. Preheat your grill for indirect cooking at 150°F
2. Place a saucepan over the grates, add all your ingredients, and allow to boil.
3. Reduce smoker temperature and allow the sauce to simmer for 10 minutes or until the sauce is thick.

NUTRITION: Calories: 65, Carbs: 15.9g, Fat: 1.3g, Protein: 2.1g

Bourbon Whiskey Sauce

Preparation time: 20 Minutes
Cooking time: 25 Minutes
Servings: 3 Cups

INGREDIENTS:

- 2 cups ketchup
- 1/4 cup Worcestershire sauce
- 3/4 cup bourbon whiskey
- 1/3 cup apple cider vinegar
- 1/2 onion, minced
- 1/4 cup of tomato paste
- 2 cloves of garlic, minced
- 1/2 Tsp. Black pepper
- 1/2 cup brown sugar
- 1/2 Tbsp. Salt
- Hot pepper sauce to taste
- 1 Tbsp. Liquid smoke flavoring

DIRECTIONS:

1. Preheat your grill for indirect cooking at 150°F
2. Place a saucepan over the grates, and then add the whiskey, garlic, and onions.
3. Simmer until the onion is translucent. Then add the other ingredients and adjust the temperature to smoke. Simmer for 20 minutes. For a smooth sauce, sieve.

NUTRITION: Calories: 107kcal, Carbs: 16.6g, Fat: 1.8g, Protein: 0.8g

Texas-Style Brisket Run

Preparation time: 5 Minutes
Cooking time: 0 Minutes
Servings: 1

INGREDIENTS:

- 2 Tsp. Sugar
- 2 Tbsp. Kosher salt
- 2 Tsp. Chili powder
- 2 Tbsp. Black pepper
- 2 Tbsp. Cayenne pepper
- 2 Tbsp. Powdered garlic
- 2 Tsp. Grounded cumin
- 2 Tbsp. Powdered onions
- 1/4 cup paprika, smoked

DIRECTIONS:

1. Put and combine all the ingredients in a small bowl until it is well blended.
2. Transfer to an airtight jar or container. Store in a cool place.

NUTRITION: Calories: 18kcal, Carbs: 2g, Fat: 1g, Protein: 0.6g

Pork Dry Rub

Preparation time: 5 Minutes
Cooking time: 0 Minutes
Servings: 1 Cup

INGREDIENTS:

- 1 Tbsp. Kosher salt
- 2 Tbsp. Powered onions
- 1 Tbsp. Cayenne pepper
- 1 Tsp. Dried mustard
- 1/4 cup brown sugar
- 1 Tbsp. Powdered garlic
- 1 Tbsp. Powdered chili pepper
- 1/4 cup smoked paprika
- 2 Tbsp. Black pepper

DIRECTIONS:

1. Set all the ingredients in a bowl.
2. Transfer to an airtight jar or container.
3. Keep stored in a cool, dry place.

NUTRITION: Calories: 16kcal, Carbs: 3g, Fat: 0.9g, Protein: 0.8g

Brown Sugar Rub

Preparation time: 10 minutes
Cooking time: 0 minute
Servings: 3 tablespoons

INGREDIENTS:

- 2 tablespoons light brown sugar
- 1 teaspoon coarse kosher salt
- 1 teaspoon garlic powder
- 1 teaspoon onion powder
- 1 teaspoon sweet paprika
- 1/2 teaspoon freshly ground black pepper
- 1/2 teaspoon cayenne pepper
- 1/2 teaspoon dried oregano leaves
- 1/4 teaspoon smoked paprika

DIRECTIONS:

1. Brown sugar, salt, garlic powder, onion powder, sweet paprika, black pepper, cayenne, oregano, and smoked paprika should all be combined in an airtight container or zip-top bag.
2. Shake to combine after sealing the container. An airtight jar can preserve the leftover rub for months.

NUTRITION: Calories: 62, Carbs: 15.9g, Fat: 0.3g, Protein: 0.1g

Texas Barbeque Rub

Preparation time: 5 Minutes
Cooking time: 0 Minutes
Servings: 1/2 cup

INGREDIENTS:

- 1 Tsp. Sugar
- 1 Tbsp. Seasoned salt
- 1 Tbsp. Black pepper
- 1 Tsp. Chili powder
- 1 Tbsp. Powdered onions
- 1 Tbsp. Smoked paprika
- 1 Tsp. Sugar
- 1 Tbsp. Powdered garlic

DIRECTIONS:

1. Run all the ingredients into a bowl and mix thoroughly.
2. Keep stored in an airtight jar or container.

NUTRITION: Calories: 22kcal, Carbs: 2g, Fat: 0.2g, Protein: 0.6g

Chicken Marinade

Preparation time: 5 Minutes
Cooking time: 0 Minutes
Servings: 3 Cups

INGREDIENTS:

- halved chicken breast (bone and skin removed)
- 1 Tbsp. Spicy brown mustard
- 2/3 cup of soy sauce
- 1 Tsp. Powdered garlic
- 2 Tbsp. Liquid smoke flavoring
- 2/3 cup extra virgin olive oil
- 2/3 cup lemon juice
- 2 Tsp. Black pepper

DIRECTIONS:

1. Set all the ingredients in a bowl.
2. Run the chicken into the bowl and allow it to marinate for about 3- 4hours in the refrigerator. Remove the chicken, then smoke, grill, or roast the chicken.

NUTRITION: Calories: 507kcal, Carbs: 46.6g, Fat: 41.8g, Protein: 28g

Barbeque Sauce

Preparation time: 5 Minutes
Cooking time: 0 Minutes
Servings: 2 Cups

INGREDIENTS:

- 1/4 cup of water
- 1/4 cup red wine vinegar
- 1 Tbsp. Worcestershire sauce
- 1 Tsp. Paprika
- 1 Tsp. Salt
- 1 Tbsp. Dried mustard
- 1 Tsp. black pepper
- 1 cup ketchup
- 1 cup brown sugar

DIRECTIONS:

1. Process all the ingredients into a bowl, one after the other.
2. Process until they are evenly mixed.
3. Transfer the sauce to a closed-lid jar. Store in the refrigerator.

NUTRITION: Calories: 43kcal, Carbs: 10g, Fat: 0.3g, Protein: 0.9g

Carolina Gold BBQ Sauce

Preparation time: 5 Minutes
Cooking time: 0 Minutes
Servings: 2 Cups

INGREDIENTS:

- 1 cup yellow mustard
- 1/2 cup apple cider vinegar
- 1/4 cup honey
- 1 tablespoon dark brown sugar
- 2 teaspoons Worcestershire sauce
- 1 teaspoon hot sauce

DIRECTIONS:

1. Set all ingredients in a bowl and mix until evenly combined.

NUTRITION: Calories: 126, Sodium: 97mg, Dietary Fiber: 1.3g, Fat: 2.7g, Carbs: 22.8g, Protein: 5. 3g

Teriyaki Sauce

Preparation time: 10 Minutes
Cooking time: 0 Minutes
Servings: 4

INGREDIENTS:

- 2/3 cup soy sauce
- 1/4 cup sherry
- 2 tablespoons sugar
- 1 teaspoon ground ginger
- 1 clove garlic, finely chopped

DIRECTIONS:

1. All components should be combined in a small bowl. Before usage, whip thoroughly and let the mixture cool for an hour at room temperature.
2. To use, put your preferred meat in a plastic zipper-lock bag. Add half of the teriyaki sauce and let the food marinate for no more than twenty-four hours, but no less than an hour.

NUTRITION: Calories: 899, Sodium: 341mg, Dietary Fiber: 4.9g, Fat: 49.9g, Carbs: 99.6g, Protein: 12.7g

Thai Chili Sauce

Preparation time: 10 Minutes
Cooking time: 0 Minutes
Servings: 4

INGREDIENTS:

- 1 cup water
- 1 cup rice vinegar
- 1 cup sugar
- 2 teaspoons freshly grated ginger
- 1 teaspoon garlic, finely chopped
- 2 teaspoons hot chili pepper, chopped
- 2 teaspoons ketchup
- 2 teaspoons cornstarch

DIRECTIONS:

1. Water and vinegar should be combined in a medium pot. Add the sugar, ginger, garlic, chili pepper, and ketchup after bringing it to a boil.
2. Add the corn starch after five minutes on medium heat.
3. Before using or storing, remove the pan from the heat and let it cool fully.

NUTRITION: Calories: 761, Sodium: 54mg, Dietary Fiber: 3.1g, Fat: 36.1g, Carbs: 105.1g, Protein: 3.9g.

Easy Jerk Seasoning

Preparation time: 10 Minutes
Cooking time: 0 Minutes
Servings: 1

INGREDIENTS:

- 2 tablespoons dried minced onion
- 2 and a half teaspoons dried thyme
- 2 teaspoons ground allspice
- 1/2 teaspoon cayenne pepper
- 1/2 teaspoon salts
- 2 tablespoons vegetable oil
- 2 teaspoons ground black pepper
- 1/2 teaspoon ground cinnamon

DIRECTIONS:

1. In a small basin, stir together the thyme, salt, dried onion, allspice, cayenne pepper, and cinnamon. Rub spice onto the meat after gently coating it with oil.

NUTRITION: Calories: 43kcal, Carbs: 10g, Fat: 0.3g, Protein: 0.9g

Pork

Smoked Baby Back Ribs

Preparation time: 10 minutes
Cooking time: 2 hours
Servings: 6
Preferred Wood Pellet: Hickory

INGREDIENTS:

- 3 racks baby back ribs
- Salt and pepper to taste

DIRECTIONS:

1. Remove the excess membrane that covers the ribs to clean them. The ribs are pat dried with a fresh paper towel. To taste, season the baby back ribs with salt and pepper. Before cooking, let the food rest in the refrigerator for at least 4 hours.
2. Fire the grill to 225F when you're prepared to cook.
3. For 15 minutes, preheat with the lid closed.
4. For two hours, roast the ribs on the grill grate. To ensure consistent cooking, carefully turn the ribs halfway through the cooking period.

NUTRITION: Calories: 1037; Protein: 92.5g; Carbs: 1.4g; Fat: 73.7g; Sugar: 0.2g

Competition Style BBQ Pork Ribs

Preparation time: 10 minutes
Cooking time: 2 hours
Servings: 6
Preferred Wood Pellet: Hard Wood Apple

INGREDIENTS:

- 2 racks of St. Louis-style ribs
- 1 cup Traeger Pork and Poultry Rub
- 1/8 cup brown sugar
- 4 tablespoons butter
- 4 tablespoons agave
- 1 bottle Traeger Sweet and Heat BBQ Sauce

DIRECTIONS:

1. Remove the thin layer of connective tissues covering the ribs by placing them on the work surface. Brown sugar, butter, agave, and the Traeger Pork and Poultry Rub should all be combined in a separate basin. Combine well after mixing.
2. The ribs should remain in the refrigerator for at least two hours after being massaged with the rub.
3. Fire the grill to 225°F when you're ready to cook. For the ribs, roast them using your preferred wood pellets. For 15 minutes, preheat with the lid closed.
4. After placing the ribs on the barbecue grate, cover it. Smoker for 1 ½ hours. At the midway point of cooking, turn the ribs over.
5. Brush some BBQ sauce on the ribs ten minutes before the grilling is finished.
6. Slice after removing it from the grill and letting it cool.

NUTRITION: Calories: 399; Protein: 47.2g; Carbs: 3.5g; Fat: 20.5g; Sugar: 2.3g

Smoked Apple BBQ Ribs

Preparation time: 10 minutes
Cooking time: 2 hours
Servings: 6
Preferred Wood Pellet: Hard Wood Apple

INGREDIENTS:

- 2 racks St. Louis-style ribs
- 1/4 cup Traeger Big Game Rub
- 1 cup apple juice
- A bottle of Traeger BBQ Sauce

DIRECTIONS:

1. Remove the connective tissue coating covering the ribs by setting them on a work surface.
2. Mix the apple juice and game rub well in a separate basin.
3. The ribs should remain in the refrigerator for at least two hours after being massaged with the rub.
4. Fire the grill to 225F when you're ready to cook. Make the ribs using apple wood pellets. For 15 minutes, preheat with the lid closed.
5. After placing the ribs on the barbecue grate, cover it. Smoke for 1 ½ hour. At the midway point of cooking, turn the ribs over.
6. Brush some BBQ sauce on the ribs ten minutes before the grilling is finished.
7. Slice after removing it from the grill and letting it cool.

NUTRITION: Calories: 337; Protein: 47.1g; Carbs: 4.7 g; Fat: 12.9g; Sugar: 4g

Roasted Ham

Preparation time: 15 minutes
Cooking time: 2 hours 15 minutes
Servings: 6

INGREDIENTS:

- 8-10 pounds ham, bone-in
- 2 tablespoons mustard, Dijon
- 1/4 cup horseradish
- 1 bottle BBQ Apricot Sauce

DIRECTIONS:

1. Set your smoker to 325 degrees Fahrenheit.
2. The ham is placed in a roasting pan covered with foil, moved to the smoker, and smoked for one hour and thirty minutes.
3. Using a small skillet, combine the sauce, horseradish, and mustard. Cook for a few minutes at medium heat.
4. Put it to the side.
5. Glaze the ham after one and a half hours of smoking and continue smoking for 30 minutes or until the interior temperature reaches 135 degrees F.
6. Give it 20 minutes to relax. Slice, then savor!

NUTRITION: Calories: 460, Fats: 43g, Carbs: 10g, Fiber: 1g

Smoked Pork Loin

Preparation time: 15 minutes
Cooking time: 3 hours
Servings: 6
Preferred Wood Pellet: Hickory

INGREDIENTS:

- 1/2 quart apple juice
- 1/2 quart apple cider vinegar
- 1/2 cup of sugar
- 1/4 cup of salt
- 2 tablespoons fresh ground pepper
- 1 pork loin roast
- 1/2 cup Greek seasoning

DIRECTIONS:

1. Make the brine mixture in a big container by mixing apple juice, vinegar, salt, pepper, sugar, and liquid smoke.
2. When necessary, add extra water.
3. Overnight, cover and chill.
4. Set your smoker's temperature to 250 degrees Fahrenheit.
5. Place the meat in your smoker after seasoning it with Greek seasoning.
6. Smoker for 3 hours or until the thickest section reaches a temperature of 160 degrees Fahrenheit.
7. Dispense and savor!

NUTRITION: Calories: 169, Fats: 5g, Carbs: 3g, Fiber: 3g

Smoke Pulled Pork

Preparation time: 15 minutes
Cooking time: 3 hours
Servings: 4
Preferred Wood Pellet: Hard Wood Apple

INGREDIENTS:

- 6-9 lb. of whole pork shoulder
- 2 cups of apple cider
- Big game rub

DIRECTIONS

1. Set the smoker to preheat at 250 degrees Fahrenheit for 15 minutes with the lid closed.
2. Now trim the pork's butt of any extra fat and season it with big game spice.
3. Place the pork butt on the grill grate with the fat side facing up.
4. Smoke it until the inside reaches 160 degrees Fahrenheit. About three to five hours should pass for this.
5. It should be taken off the grill and set aside.
6. Now place 4 huge sheets of aluminum foil, one on top of the other, on a large baking sheet. This need to be large enough to completely around the pork butt.
7. Keep the pork butt in the middle of the foil and slightly raise the edges. Pour apple cider over the meat and securely enclose it.
8. Maintains it on the grill while cooking with the fat side facing up.
9. It should be taken off the grill and rest in the foil pouch for 45 minutes.

10. Remove the foil, then drain any excess liquid.
11. Remove the bones and extra fat from the pork and store it in a dish.
12. Re-season the pork with the big game seasoning after adding the separated liquid.
13. Offer and savor

NUTRITION: Calories: 169, Fats: 5g, Carbs: 3g, Fiber: 3g

Barbecue Baby Back Ribs

Preparation time: 15 minutes
Cooking time: 4 hours
Servings: 2
Preferred Wood Pellet: Apricot or Alder

INGREDIENTS:

- 2 full slabs baby back ribs, back membranes removed
- 1 cup prepared table mustard
- 1 cup Pork Rub
- 1 cup apple juice, divided
- 1 cup packed light brown sugar, divided
- 1 cup of The Ultimate BBQ Sauce, divided

DIRECTIONS:

1. Provide wood pellets for your smoker and follow the manufacturer's instructions for starting it up. Preheat to 150°F (66°C) to 180°F (82°C), or to the "Smoke" setting, with the lid closed.
2. Apply mustard on the ribs to make the rub stay and keep the moisture in.
3. Gently massage in the rub.
4. Remove the ribs, then carefully wrap each rack in foil. Add 1/2 cup apple juice and 1/2 cup brown sugar to each box before carefully sealing.
5. Add the foil-wrapped ribs to the grill, cover them, and let them smoke for two more hours.
6. Remove the foil from the ribs and carefully unfold them. Each rib should be covered with 1/2 cup of barbecue sauce before continuing to smoke for 30 to 1 hour with the lid closed or until the meat is tender and has a reddish peel.

NUTRITION: Calories: 764, Fat: 55g, Carbohydrates: 2g, Protein: 63g

Maple Baby Back Ribs

Preparation time: 5 minutes
Cooking time: 3 hours
Servings: 2
Preferred Wood Pellet: Apricot or Alder

INGREDIENTS:

- 2 (2- or 3-pound / 907- or 1360-g) racks baby back ribs
- 2 tablespoons yellow mustard
- 1 batch Sweet Brown Sugar Rub
- 1/2 cup maple syrup, divided
- 2 tablespoons light brown sugar
- 1 cup Pepsi or another non-diet cola
- 1/4 cup The Ultimate BBQ Sauce

DIRECTIONS:

1. Provide wood pellets for your smoker and follow the manufacturer's instructions for starting it up.
2. Take off the membrane covering the ribs' undersides. To do this, make an X-shaped incision through the membrane, then use a paper towel to peel it away from the ribs.
3. Apply mustard to both sides of the ribs and season with the rub.
4. For three hours, place the ribs in the smoker at 225°F
5. Remove the ribs and set them, bone-side up, on a sheet of aluminum foil that is large enough to fully enclose the ribs. Repeat applying the brown sugar and maple syrup to the meat side of the ribs after turning them over.
6. The grill's temperature should be raised to 300°F (149°C).

7. Combine the remaining 6 tablespoons of maple syrup with the barbecue sauce. To baste the ribs, use this. Without the foil, place the ribs back on the grill and cook for an additional 15 minutes to caramelize the sauce.
8. Serve right after being cut into individual ribs.

NUTRITION: Calories: 214, Fat: 45, Carbohydrates: 12g, Protein: 43g

Smoked Mustard Baby Back Ribs

Preparation time: 2 5 minutes
Cooking time: 6 hours
Servings: 2
Preferred Wood Pellet: Apricot or Alder

INGREDIENTS:

- 2 (2- or 3-pound / 907- or 1360-g) racks baby back ribs
- 2 tablespoons yellow mustard
- 1 batch Pork Rub

DIRECTIONS:

1. Provide wood pellets for your smoker and follow the manufacturer's instructions for starting it up.
2. Take off the membrane covering the ribs' undersides. To do this, make an X-shaped incision through the membrane, then use a paper towel to peel it away from the ribs.
3. Set your wood pellet barbecue to 225 degrees Fahrenheit and start smoking for three hours.
4. Apply mustard to both sides of the ribs and season with the rub.
5. The ribs should be prepared and smoked until they reach a temperature of 190F.
6. Cut each rib up separately. Serve right away.

NUTRITION: Calories: 214, Fat: 45g, Carbohydrates: 12g, Protein: 43g

Grilled Pork Chops

Preparation time: 10 minutes
Cooking time: 1 hour 5 minutes
Servings: 4
Preferred Wood Pellet: Hickory

INGREDIENTS:

- 4 centers cut boneless pork chops
- 2 Tbsp. olive oil

Rub:
- 1 Tsp. kosher salt or to taste
- 1 Tsp. Italian seasoning
- 1 Tsp. Greek seasoning
- 1/2 Tsp. cayenne pepper
- 2 Tsp. brown sugar
- 1 Tsp. finely chopped fresh rosemary
- 1 Tsp. ground black pepper
- 1 Tsp. dried basil
- 1/2 Tsp. peppermint
- 1/2 Tsp. oregano
- 1/2 Tsp. ground cumin

DIRECTIONS:

1. Set your grill on the smoke setting and keep the lid open until the fire goes.
2. Set the grill to 180°F.
3. In a small mixing bowl, combine all of the rub's components.
4. Apply oil to the pork chops' whole surface area. Sprinkle the rub liberally on both sides of each pork chop.

5. Place the pork chops on the grill and let them smoke for 45 minutes with the lid closed.
6. After removing the pork chops from the grill, turn the heat to 450 degrees.
7. The pork chops should be placed back on the grill and smoked for an additional 20 minutes, or until the internal temperature reaches 150°F.
8. After removing the pork chop from the grill, give it some time to rest.
9. Slice and serve.

NUTRITION: Calories: 216, Fat: 11.6g, Cholesterol: 76mg, Carbohydrate: 2.9g, Protein: 25.2g

Lemon Pepper Pork Tenderloin

Preparation time: 20 minutes
Cooking time: 20 minutes
Servings: 6
Preferred Wood Pellet: Apricot or Alder

INGREDIENTS:

- 2 pounds pork tenderloin, fat trimmed

For the Marinade:
- 1/2 teaspoon minced garlic
- 2 lemons, zester
- 1 teaspoon minced parsley
- 1/2 teaspoon salt
- 1/4 teaspoon ground black pepper
- 1 teaspoon lemon juice
- 2 tablespoons olive oil

DIRECTIONS:

1. Take a small bowl, add all the ingredients, and mix to combine to make the marinade.
2. Meat tenderloin should be placed in a big plastic bag with the marinade, sealed, and turned upside down to coat the pork. The pork should marinate for at least two hours in the refrigerator.
3. Put apple-flavored wood pellets in the grill hopper, turn the grill on using the control panel, choose "smoke" from the temperature dial, or preheat the grill for at least 15 minutes at 375 degrees.
4. Open the grill's lid after it has heated up, add the pork tenderloin to the grill grate, cover it, and smoke the meat

for 20 minutes, flipping it halfway through, until the internal temperature reaches 145°F.
5. Place the pork on a cutting board, let it rest for ten minutes, then slice it and serve.

NUTRITION: Calories: 288, Fat: 16.6g, Carbs: 6.2g, Protein: 26.4g

Chinese BBQ Pork

Preparation time: 10 minutes
Cooking time: 2 hours
Servings: 8
Preferred Wood Pellet: Apricot or Alder

INGREDIENTS:

- 2 pork tenderloins, silver skin removed

For the Marinade:
- 1/2 teaspoon minced garlic
- 1 1/2 tablespoon brown sugar
- 1 teaspoon Chinese five-spice
- 1/4 cup honey
- 1 tablespoon Asian sesame oil
- 1/4 cup hoisin sauce
- 2 teaspoons red food coloring
- 1 tablespoon oyster sauce, optional
- 3 tablespoons soy sauce

For the Five-Spice Sauce:
- 1/4 teaspoon Chinese five-spice
- 3 tablespoons brown sugar
- 1 teaspoon yellow mustard
- 1/4 cup ketchup

DIRECTIONS:

1. Take a small bowl, add all the ingredients, and mix to combine to make the marinade.
2. Meat tenderloin should be placed in a big plastic bag with the marinade, sealed, and turned upside down to coat the

pork. The pork should marinate for at least 8 hours in the refrigerator.

3. Put some maple-flavored wood pellets in the grill hopper, turn the grill on with the control panel, choose "smoke" on the temperature dial, or set the temperature to 225°F and wait at least five minutes before using it.
4. Remove the pork from the marinade, pour the marinade into a small saucepan, heat it for 3 minutes over medium-high heat, and then put it aside to cool.
5. Open the grill's lid after it has heated up, add the pork to the grill grate, close it, and smoke the meat for two hours, basting once halfway through.
6. Take a small saucepan, set it over low heat, add all the ingredients, and whisk until everything is properly blended to make the five- spice sauce. After the sugar has dissolved and been heated through and thickened, leave it aside until you need it.
7. When the pork is finished, put it on a plate and allow it to rest for 15 minutes. In the meanwhile, raise the grill's smoking temperature to 450°F and let it prepare for at least 10 minutes.
8. To gently brown the pork, place it back on the grill grate and cook for 3 minutes on each side.
9. Serve the pork with the prepared five-spice sauce after transferring it to a plate and resting it for five minutes.

NUTRITION: Calories: 280, Fat: 8g, Carbs: 12g, Protein: 40g

Beef

Wholesome Beef Tri-Tip

Preparation time: 1 hour
Cooking time: 2 hours
Servings: 4
Preferred Wood Pellet: Oak or Alder

INGREDIENTS:

- 2-3 pounds beef tri-tip roast
- 1/2 teaspoon garlic powder
- 1 teaspoon onion powder
- 1 teaspoon espresso powder
- 1 teaspoon brown sugar
- 1 teaspoon black pepper
- 1-1 /2 teaspoon mild chili powder
- 2 teaspoons salt

DIRECTIONS:

1. Take a small-sized bowl and add all of the rub ingredients
2. Transfer roast to a cutting board and slice up any fat cap, score the fat
3. Turn the roast 90 degrees and score in diamond patterns
4. Season meat all over using the rub, making sure to press it well to coat it
5. Place roast on the side and let it sit for 30-60 minutes
6. Take your drip pan and add water; cover it with aluminum foil. Preheat your smoker to 225°F
7. Use water to fill water pan halfway through and place it over the drip pan. Add wood chips to the side tray
8. Place your tri-tip (Fat side up) on your middle rack of the smoker, close the door and let it smoke for 2 hours until the internal temperature reaches 130-135 degrees F

9. Transfer roast to a cutting board and make a tent with foil. Let it sit for 20 minutes
10. Slice evenly and serve
11. Enjoy!

NUTRITION: Calories: 764, Fat: 55g, Carbohydrates: 2g, Protein: 63g

Meat Chuck Short Rib

Preparation time: 20 Minutes
Cooking time: 5-6 Hours
Servings: 2
Preferred Wood Pellet: Mesquite or Hickory Pellets

INGREDIENTS:

- English cut 4 bone slab beef chuck short rib
- 3-4 cups of mustard yellow mustard or extra virgin olive oil
- 3-5 tablespoons of Western Love

DIRECTIONS:

1. Remove the silvery skin and trim the fat cap off the rib bone, leaving 1/4 inch of fat behind.
2. To raise the piece of meat and properly season it, take the membrane from the bone and slide the spoon handle under the membrane. A paper towel may be used to grab the membrane and peel it away from the bone.
3. The short rib slab should be covered with mustard or olive oil on both sides. You may season all sides by rubbing it.
4. Heat the grill and wood pellet smoker to 225 °F using indirect heating.
5. The thickest area of the rib bone plank should be inserted into a wood pellet smoker, grill, or remote meat probe. If your grill doesn't have a meat probe or you don't have a remote meat probe, check the interior temperature of the food while it cooks using an instant-reading digital thermometer.
6. The short rib bone should be placed on the grill with the bone side down and smoked for 5 hours at 225 °F.

7. After five hours, if the internal temperature of the ribs has not risen to at least 195 °F, raise the pit temperature to 250 °F and continue cooking the ribs until they are between 195 ° and 205 °F.
8. Before serving, place the smoked short rib bone in the loose foil tent for 15 minutes.

NUTRITION: Calories: 357, Carbs: 0g, Fat: 22g, Protein: 37g

Reverse-Seared Tri-Tip

Preparation time: 10 minutes
Cooking time: 3 hours
Servings: 4
Preferred Wood Pellet: Apricot or Alder

INGREDIENTS:

- 1 1/2 pounds tri-tip roast
- 1 batch Espresso Brisket Rub

DIRECTIONS:

1. Supply your smoker with wood pellets and follow the manufacturer's specific start-up procedure. Let the grill preheat, with the lid closed, to 180°F.
2. Season the tri-tip roast with the rub. With your two hands, work the rub into the meat.
3. Place the meat to roast directly on the grill grate and smoke until its internal temperature reaches 140°F.
4. Increase the grill's temperature to 450°F and cook until the roast's internal temperature reaches 145°F.
5. Remove the tri-tip roast from the grill and rest 10 to 15 minutes before slicing and serving.

NUTRITION: Calories: 290, Carbs: 5g, Fat: 18g, Protein: 30g

George's Smoked Tri-Tip

Preparation time: 25 minutes
Cooking time: 5 hours
Servings: 4
Preferred Wood Pellet: Apricot or Alder

INGREDIENTS:

- 11/2 pounds tri-tip roast
- Salt
- Freshly ground black pepper
- 2 teaspoons garlic powder
- 2 teaspoons lemon pepper
- 1/2 cup apple juice

DIRECTIONS:

1. Provide wood pellets for your smoker and fire them up according to the manufacturer's instructions. Allow your grill to heat to 180°F with the lid closed.
2. Salt, pepper, garlic powder, and lemon pepper should be used to season the tri-tip roast. Work the spice into the meat with your two hands.
3. Directly on the grill grate, place the meat to be roasted, and let it smoke for four hours.
4. Remove the tri-tip from the grill and cover it thoroughly in aluminum foil.
5. The grill's temperature should be raised to 375°F.
6. Around the roast, fold the foil in on three sides, then pour the apple juice. To fully enclose the tri-tip and liquid, fold the last edge in. Place the tri-tip back on the grill and let it cook for an additional 45 minutes.

7. Before opening, slicing, and serving, remove the tri-tip roast from the grill and allow it to rest for 10 to 15 minutes.

NUTRITION: Calories: 155, Carbs: 0g, Fat: 7g, Protein: 23g

Pulled Beef

Preparation time: 25 minutes
Cooking time: 12 to 14 hours
Servings: 5 to 8
Preferred Wood Pellet: Apricot or Alder

INGREDIENTS:

- 1 (4-pound) top round roast
- 2 tablespoons yellow mustard
- 1 batch Espresso Brisket Rub
- 1/2 cup beef broth

DIRECTIONS:

1. Provide wood pellets for your smoker and fire them up according to the manufacturer's instructions. To produce high-quality food, let your griller warm with the lid closed at 225°F.
2. Apply mustard over the top, round roast and season with the rub. Work the rub into the meat with both hands.
3. Roasting meat should be placed directly on the grill grate and smoked until it reaches 160°F inside and develops a black bark.
4. After removing the roast from the grill, cover it thoroughly in aluminum foil.
5. 350°F should now be the grill's temperature.
6. Around the roast, fold the foil in on three sides, then pour the beef broth. The last side should be folded to fully enclose the roast and liquid. Bring the roast back to the grill and cook it there until the internal temperature reaches 195 degrees Fahrenheit.

7. After removing the roast from the grill, put it in a cooler. Let the roast rest for a couple of hours with the cooler covered.
8. Your roast should be taken out of the cooler and unwrapped. You can dissect the meat with your fingertips alone. Serve right away.

NUTRITION: Calories: 213, Carbs: 0g, Fat: 16g, Protein: 15g

La Rochelle Steak

Preparation time: 10 minutes
Cooking time: 20 minutes
Servings: 4
Preferred Wood Pellet: Hard Wood Mesquite

INGREDIENTS:

- 1 tablespoon red currant jelly
- 1/2 teaspoon salt
- 3 teaspoon curry powder
- 8 ounces pineapple chunks in juice
- 1 1/2 pounds flank steak
- 1/4 cup olive oil

DIRECTIONS:

1. The flank steak should be placed in a big bag.
2. Combine the olive oil, pineapple chunks, red currant jelly, pepper, salt, and curry powder.
3. Place the flank steak on top of this mixture.
4. Place for four hours in the refrigerator.
5. Follow your cooker's starting instructions after adding wood pellets to your smoker. Close the cover of your smoker while preheating it to 350 degrees.
6. When cooking the steak, take it out of the fridge 30 minutes beforehand.
7. The steaks should grill for 10 minutes on each side or until done to your preference after being placed on the grill, covered.
8. Take your roasted food off the grill and let it cool for 10 minutes.

NUTRITION: Calories: 200, Carbs: 0g, Fat: 7g, Protein: 33g

Brined Smoked Brisket

Preparation time: 30 Minutes
Cooking time: 7 Hours 30 minutes
Servings: 6
Preferred Wood Pellet: Hard Wood Mesquite

INGREDIENTS:

- 1 cup brown sugar
- 1/2 cup of salt
- One flat cut brisket
- 1/4 cup Traeger Beef Rub

DIRECTIONS:

1. Melt the sugar and salt in 6 quarts of boiling water to create the brine.
2. Place the brisket in the solution after allowing it to cool at room temperature.
3. Place the stock in the refrigerator and marinate for 12 hours.
4. The brisket should be taken out of the brine and dried with paper towels.
5. Add some Traeger Beef Rub and rub it until all surfaces are covered.
6. Fire up the grill to 250F when you're ready to cook.
7. After covering the pot, let it cook for 15 minutes.
8. The brisket should be put on the grill grates and cooked for four hours.
9. Cook the brisket for a further three hours at 275F after wrapping it twice in foil.
10. The brisket should be unwrapped and grilled for another 30 minutes.
11. Before cutting it, let it cool.

NUTRITION: Calories: 364, Protein: 48.7 g, Carbs: 16.6g, Fat: 11.6g, Sugar: 12.3g

Cocoa-Rubbed Steak for Two

Preparation time: 50 minutes
Cooking time: 1 hour
Servings: 4
Preferred Wood Pellet: Apricot or Alder

INGREDIENTS:

- 2 whole rib-eye roast, trimmed
- 1 cup Traeger Coffee Rub
- 1/4 cup cocoa powder

DIRECTIONS:

1. Slice the roast into 2 1/2 inches thick. 2 steaks that should be set away and frozen for later use.
2. In a dish, combine the cocoa powder and Traeger Coffee Rub. The rub mixture may be used to mildly season the steaks. The leftover rub mixture should be saved for subsequent use.
3. Set your smoker to 225°F and leave the lid off for 15 minutes.
4. Use Traeger Beef Rub to season the steaks.
5. Place the meats on the grill and let them smoke for an hour.
6. The steaks should be taken from the grill and let to rest.
7. Before serving, remove the steaks and let them cool for 5 minutes.

NUTRITION: Calories: 764, Fat: 55g, Carbohydrates: 2g, Protein: 63g

Smoked Rib-Eye Caps

Preparation time: 5 minutes
Cooking time: 1 hour
Servings: 4
Preferred Wood Pellet: Apricot or Alder

INGREDIENTS:

- 1 1/2 pounds (680 g) rib-eye cap, trimmed
- 2 tablespoons Traeger Beef Rub
- 2 tablespoons Traeger Coffee Rub

DIRECTIONS:

1. Roll the cap into steaks after slicing it into 4 equal sections. To fasten, tie with butcher's twine.
2. The steaks should be gently seasoned with the rub mixture after combining the two rubs in a small dish.
3. Set your smoker to 225°F and leave the lid off for 15 minutes.
4. Use Traeger Beef Rub to season the steaks.
5. Place the steaks on the grill and let them smoke for an hour.
6. The steaks should be taken from the grill and let to rest.
7. Before serving, remove the steaks and let them cool for 5 minutes.

NUTRITION: Calories: 764, Fat: 50g, Carbohydrates: 21g

Seared Rib-Eye Steaks

Preparation time: 5 minutes
Cooking time: 1 hour
Servings: 2
Preferred Wood Pellet: Apricot or Alder

INGREDIENTS:

- 2 (1 1/2 inch thick) rib-eye steaks
- Meat Church Gourmet Garlic and Herb Seasoning
- Meat Church Holy Cow BBQ Rub
- 2 tablespoons butter

DIRECTIONS:

1. Preheat your smoker to 225°F, lid closed for 15 minutes.
2. Season the steaks with Traeger Beef Rub.
3. Arrange the steaks directly on the grill and smoke for 60 minutes.
4. Remove the steaks from the grill and set them aside to rest.
5. Take out the steaks and cool for 5 minutes before serving.

NUTRITION: Calories: 764, Fat: 55g, Carbohydrates: 2g, Protein: 63g

BBQ Brisket with Coffee Rub

Preparation time: 20 Minutes
Cooking time: 9 Hours
Servings: 10
Preferred Wood Pellet: Hard Wood Mesquite

INGREDIENTS:

- 5 pounds whole packer brisket
- Two tablespoons Traeger Coffee Rub
- 1 cup of water
- Two tablespoons salt

DIRECTIONS:

1. Trim the brisket and remove any membrane.
2. Leave a 1/4" inch gap on the bottom.
3. Mix the coffee rub, water, and salt in a bowl until dissolved.
4. Season the brisket with the spice rub and allow it to rest in the fridge for 3 hours.
5. When ready to cook, fire the grill to 250F.
6. Close the lid and heat up for 15 minutes.
7. Move the brisket on the grill grate and close the lid.
8. Cook for 6 hours or up until the internal temperature reaches 160F.
9. Wrap the brisket in aluminum foil and increase the temperature to 275F.
10. Cook for another 3 hours.

NUTRITION: Calories: 352, Protein: 47g, Carbs: 0g, Fat: 16.7g, Sugar: 0g

Smoked Texas BBQ Brisket

Preparation time: 30 Minutes
Cooking time: 5 Hours
Servings: 4
Preferred Wood Pellet: Mesquite

INGREDIENTS:

- 6 pounds whole packer brisket
- Commercial BBQ rub of your choice

DIRECTIONS:

1. Remove any membranes from the brisket and trim the fat.
2. Cut the fat side to a thickness of 1/4 inch.
3. After applying the BBQ rub to all of the brisket's edges, let it rest in the refrigerator for 30 minutes.
4. Fire up the grill to 250F when you're ready to cook.
5. After sealing the cover, cook the food for 15 minutes.
6. When the brisket's internal temperature reaches 165°F, place it on the grill grates and let it cook for five hours.
7. After cooking, take the brisket off the grill and let it rest before slicing.

NUTRITION: Calories: 703, Protein: 93.9g, Carbs: 0 g, Fat: 33.4g, Sugar: 0g

Pastrami Short Ribs

Preparation time: 30 Minutes
Cooking time: 3 Hours 30 minutes
Servings: 4
Preferred Wood Pellet: Hard Wood Apple

INGREDIENTS:

- 2 quarts water
- 1/3 cup salt
- Two teaspoons pink salt
- 1/4 cup brown sugar
- Four garlic
- Four tablespoons coriander seeds
- Three tablespoons peppercorns
- Two teaspoons mustard seeds
- Two tablespoons extra virgin olive oil
- One large ginger ale
- 2 pounds beef short ribs

DIRECTIONS:

1. In a large bowl, combine all the ingredients except the oil, ginger ale, and short ribs.
2. Mix everything well. Add the short ribs in last.
3. For at least 12 hours, let the short ribs marinate in the refrigerator.
4. Fire up the grill to 300F when you're ready to cook.
5. After covering the pot, let it cook for 15 minutes.
6. Short ribs should be placed on the grill grates and smoked for two hours. Put some oil on.
7. Bring the ribs to a roasting pan and cover them with enough ginger ale.

8. Wrap foil around the pan.
9. Place in the grill, increase the temperature to 350F and cook for 1 1/2 hours.

NUTRITION: Calories: 521, Protein: 46.7g, Carbs: 16.9g, Fat: 30.1g, Sugar: 13.7g

Poultry

Buffalo Chicken Wings

Preparation time: 15 Minutes
Cooking time: 25 Minutes
Preferred Wood Pellet: Oak or Alder
Servings: 6

INGREDIENTS:

- 2 lb. chicken wings
- 1/2 cup sweet, spicy dry rub
- 2/3 cup buffalo sauce
- Celery, chopped

DIRECTIONS:

1. Start your wood pellet grill.
2. Set it to 450 degrees F.
3. Sprinkle the chicken wings with the dry rub.
4. Place on the grill rack.
5. Cook for 10 minutes per side.
6. Brush with buffalo sauce.
7. Grill for another 5 minutes.
8. Dip each wing in the buffalo sauce.
9. Sprinkle the celery on top.

NUTRITION: Calories 935, Total fat 53g, Saturated fat 15g, Protein 107g, Sodium 320mg

Sweet and Sour Chicken

Preparation time: 30 Minutes
Cooking time: 3 Hours
Servings: 4
Preferred Wood Pellet: Oak or Alder

INGREDIENTS:

- Eight chicken drumsticks
- 1/4 cup soy sauce
- 1 cup ketchup
- Two tablespoons rice wine vinegar
- Two tablespoons lemon juice
- Two tablespoons honey
- Two tablespoons garlic, minced
- Two tablespoons ginger, minced
- One tablespoon sweet-spicy dry rub
- Three tablespoons brown sugar

DIRECTIONS:

1. Add all the sauce ingredients.
2. Mix thoroughly.
3. Refrigerate after transferring half of the mixture to another bowl.
4. To the bowl with the remaining sauce, add the chicken.
5. Evenly coat by tossing.
6. For 4 hours, cover and chill.
7. Start the grill using wood pellets.
8. Make it smoke.
9. Set the thermostat to 225 degrees Fahrenheit.

10. For three hours, smoke the chicken.

11. Serve the chicken with the sauce that was set aside.

NUTRITION: Calories 935, Total fat 53g, Saturated fat 15g, Protein 107g, Sodium 320mg

Smoked Chicken with Perfect Poultry Rub

Preparation time: 20 minutes
Cooking time: 3 hours 15 minutes.
Servings: 2
Preferred Wood Pellet: Apricot or Alder

INGREDIENTS:

- 2 Tbsp. of onion, powder
- 1/4 cup of black pepper, freshly ground
- 2 Tbsp. of dry mustard
- 3/4 cup of paprika
- 4pound chicken
- 2 lemons
- 2 Tsp. of cayenne
- 1/4 cup of sugar
- 1/4 cup of celery salt

DIRECTIONS:

1. Combine the onion powder, paprika, black pepper, cayenne, dry mustard, celery, salt, sugar, and 2 lemons in a bowl.
2. Slice some of the chicken before adding it to the rub so the flavors can penetrate.
3. Preheat the grill for 15 minutes at 225°F.
4. The chicken should be smoked for three hours or until it reaches an internal temperature of 160°F on the prepared grill.
5. After the chicken has cooled, serve it.

NUTRITION: Calories: 255kcal, Protein: 35g, Carbs: 42g, Fat: 35g.

Chicken Lollipops

Preparation time: 30 Minutes
Cooking time: 2 Hours 15 minutes
Servings: 6
Preferred Wood Pellet: Oak or Alder

INGREDIENTS:

- 12 chicken lollipops
- Chicken seasoning
- Ten tablespoons butter, sliced into 12 cubes
- 1 cup barbecue sauce
- 1 cup hot sauce

DIRECTIONS:

1. Start the grill using wood pellets.
2. Set the temperature to 300 F.
3. Then use the chicken seasoning to season the chicken.
4. Put the chicken on a baking sheet.
5. Each lollipop should have a butter cube on top of it.
6. Every 20 minutes, baste the chicken lollipops with melted butter in the pan while they cook for two hours.
7. Over the chicken, drizzle the spicy sauce and barbecue sauce.
8. For 15 minutes, grill.

NUTRITION: Calories 935, Total fat 53g, Saturated fat 15g, Protein 107g, Sodium 320mg

Asian Wings

Preparation time: 30 Minutes
Cooking time: 1 Hour 20 minutes
Servings: 6
Preferred Wood Pellet: Oak or Alder

INGREDIENTS:

- One teaspoon honey
- One teaspoon soy sauce
- Two teaspoon rice vinegar
- 1/2 cup hoisin sauce
- Two teaspoon sesame oil
- One teaspoon ginger, minced
- One teaspoon garlic, minced
- One teaspoon green onion, chopped
- 1 cup hot water
- 2 lb. chicken wings

DIRECTIONS:

1. Combine all the sauce ingredients in a large bowl. Mix well.
2. Transfer 1/3 of the sauce to another bowl and refrigerate.
3. Add the chicken wings to the remaining sauce.
4. Cover and refrigerate for 2 hours.
5. Turn on your wood pellet grill.
6. Set it to 300 degrees F.
7. Add the wings to a grilling basket. Cook for 1 hour.
8. Heat the reserved sauce in a pan.
9. Bring to a boil and then simmer for 10 minutes.

10. Brush the chicken with the remaining sauce.

11. Grill for another 10 minutes.

12. Let rest for 5 minutes before serving.

NUTRITION: Calories 935, Total fat 53g, Saturated fat 15g, Protein 107g, Sodium 320mg

Lemon Chicken in Foil Packet

Preparation time: 5 Minutes
Cooking time: 25 Minutes
Servings: 4
Preferred Wood Pellet: Oak or Alder

INGREDIENTS:

- Four chicken fillets
- Three tablespoons melted butter
- One garlic, minced
- 1-1/2 teaspoon dried Italian seasoning
- Salt and pepper to taste
- One lemon, sliced

DIRECTIONS:

1. Turn on your wood pellet grill.
2. Keep the lid open while burning for 5 minutes.
3. Preheat it to 450 degrees F.
4. Add the chicken fillet on top of the foil sheets.
5. Mix butter, garlic, seasoning, salt, and pepper in a bowl.
6. Brush the chicken with this mixture.
7. Put the lemon slices on top.
8. Wrap the chicken with the foil.
9. Grill each side for 7 to 10 minutes per side.

NUTRITION: Calories 935, Total fat 53g, Saturated fat 15g, Protein 107g, Sodium 320mg

Sweet and Spicy Chicken

Preparation time: 30 Minutes
Cooking time: 40 Minutes
Servings: 4
Preferred Wood Pellet: Oak or Alder

INGREDIENTS:

- 16 chicken wings
- Three tablespoons lime juice
- A sweet, spicy rub

DIRECTIONS:

1. Arrange chicken wings in a baking pan.
2. Pour the lime juice over the wings.
3. Sprinkle the wings with the seasoning.
4. Set your wood pellet grill to 350 degrees F.
5. Add the chicken wings to the grill.
6. Grill for 20 minutes per side.

NUTRITION: Calories 935, Total fat 53g, Saturated fat 15g, Protein 107g, Sodium 320mg

Grilled Chicken

Preparation time: 10 Minutes
Cooking time: 1 Hour and 10 Minutes
Servings: 6
Preferred Wood Pellet: Oak or Alder

INGREDIENTS:

- 5 lb. whole chicken
- 1/2 cup oil
- Traeger chicken rub

DIRECTIONS:

1. Preheat the grill with the lid open for 5 minutes. Close the lid, and let it warm for 15 minutes or until it reaches 450.
2. Use a baker's twine to tie the chicken legs, and then rub them with oil.
3. Coat the chicken with the rub and place it on the grill.
4. Cook for 70 minutes (with the lid closed).
5. Remove the chicken from the grill.

NUTRITION: Calories 935, Total fat 53g, Saturated fat 15g, Protein 107g, Sodium 320mg

Crispy and Juicy Chicken

Preparation time: 15 Minutes
Cooking time: 5 Hours
Servings: 6
Preferred Wood Pellet: Oak or Alder

INGREDIENTS:

- 3/4 C. dark brown sugar
- 1/2 C. ground espresso powder
- 1 Tbsp. ground cumin
- 1 Tbsp. ground cinnamon
- 1 Tbsp. garlic powder
- 1 Tbsp. cayenne pepper
- Salt and freshly ground black pepper
- 1 (4-lb.) whole chicken, neck and giblets removed

DIRECTIONS:

1. Set the grill to 200–225 degrees Fahrenheit and cook it for 15 minutes with the lid covered.
2. Combine brown sugar, espresso powder, spices, salt, and black pepper in a bowl.
3. Sprinkle a lot of the spice mixture on the chicken.
4. Grill the chicken for a period of three to five hours.
5. Before carving, remove the chicken from the grill and let it rest on a cutting board for approximately 10 minutes.
6. Cut the chicken into appropriately sized pieces with a sharp knife, then serve.

NUTRITION: Calories: 540, Carbohydrates: 20.7g, Protein: 88.3g, Fat: 9.6g, Sugar: 18.1g, Sodium: 226mg, Fiber: 1.2g

Glazed Chicken Thighs

Preparation time: 15 Minutes
Cooking time: 30 Minutes
Servings: 4
Preferred Wood Pellet: Oak or Alder

INGREDIENTS:

- Two garlic cloves, minced
- 1/4 C. honey
- 2 Tbsp. soy sauce
- 1/4 Tsp. red pepper flakes, crushed
- 4 (5-ounce.) skinless, boneless chicken thighs
- 2 Tbsp. olive oil
- 2 Tsp. Sweet rub
- 1/4 Tsp. red chili powder
- Freshly ground black pepper, to taste

DIRECTIONS:

1. The grill should be preheated for 15 minutes with the lid covered at 400 degrees F.
2. The garlic, honey, soy sauce, and red pepper flakes should all be mixed well in a small bowl using a wire whisk.
3. Sprinkle with black pepper, sweet rub, and chili powder after coating the chicken thighs in oil.
4. Place the chicken drumsticks on the grill, skin-side down, and cook for approximately 15 minutes.
5. Apply the garlic mixture on the thighs during the final 4-5 minutes of cooking.
6. Serve immediately.

NUTRITION: Calories: 309, Carbohydrates: 18.7g, Protein: 32.3g, Fat: 12.1g, Sugar: 17.6g, Sodium: 504mg, Fiber: 0.2g

Smoked Stuffed Avocado with Shredded Chicken

Preparation time: 15 minutes
Cooking time: 35 minutes
Servings: 10
Preferred Wood Pellet: Hard Wood Apple

INGREDIENTS:

- 3 lbs. ripe avocados

Stuffing:

- 5 cups Pulled chicken
- 2 cups Grated cheese
- 1 1/4 cups Salsa
- 20 Quail eggs

DIRECTIONS:

1. Before smoking, preheat the smoker until it reaches the appropriate temperature.
2. Remove the seeds from the ripe avocados after cutting them in half.
3. Add peach wood pellets to the hopper of a wood pellet smoker when it has warmed up. Unlock the lid.
4. Set the smoker to 375°F (191°C), then shut the lid for about 10 minutes.
5. While waiting for the smoking process, combine the salsa and cheese gratings with the pulled chicken.
6. The chicken and cheese combination should be placed on top of the avocado, leaving the center unfilled.
7. The filled avocados should be arranged in the smoker and smoked for 25 minutes.

8. Open the cover 25 minutes later.
9. Drop a cracked quail egg in the avocados' centers.
10. Once again smoke the avocado for 10 minutes or until the eggs are done.
11. Take the smoked avocados out of the smoker after it is finished, then arrange them on a serving platter.
12. Enjoy right away.

NUTRITION: Calories: 350, Fat: 20g, Carbs: 18g, Protein: 25g

Teriyaki Smoked Drumstick

Preparation time: 15 minutes (more marinade overnight)
Cooking time: 1.5 hours to 2 hours
Servings: 4
Preferred Wood Pellet: Mesquite

INGREDIENTS:

- 3 cups teriyaki marinade and cooking sauce like Yoshida's original gourmet
- Chicken seasoning 3 Tsp.
- 1 Tsp. garlic powder
- 10 chicken drumsticks

DIRECTIONS:

1. Mix the marinade and cooking sauce in a medium bowl with the chicken seasoning and garlic powder.
2. Peel off the skin of the drumstick to promote marinade penetration.
3. Make marinated chicken leg for 1 hour.
4. After 1 hour, raise the temperature to 350 ° F and cook the drumstick until the thickest part of the stick reaches an internal temperature of 180 ° F.
5. Place the chicken drumstick under the loose foil tent for 15 minutes before serving.

NUTRITION: Calories: 280, Carbs: 0g, Fat: 13g, Protein: 35g

Bacon Candy Chicken Bites

Preparation time: 30min
Cooking time: 1 hour
Servings: 6-8
Preferred Wood Pellet: Oak or Alder

INGREDIENTS:

- 16 ounce Boneless, Skinless Chicken Thighs
- 12 slices bacon (cut in half)
- 1/2 cup Brown Sugar
- 2 Tablespoon Killer Hogs The BBQ Rub
- 2 Tablespoon Sugar
- 1/2 teaspoon Cayenne Pepper

DIRECTIONS:

1. Get ready the Smoker or Grill for indirect cooking at 375.
2. Slice every thigh into chomp. Wrap each piece with 1/2 cut of bacon and secure with a toothpick.
3. Consolidate the brown sugar, barbecue rub, sugar, and cayenne in a little bowl and sprinkle over all sides of the bacon to wrap the chicken.
4. Spot the chicken thighs onto the barbecue and cook for about 45minutes or until the bacon is darker and clingy.
5. Present with your most loved plunging sauces.

NUTRITION: Calories: 71, Carbs: 0g, Fat: 2g, Protein: 12g

Monterey Chicken

Preparation time: 5 minutes
Cooking time: 20 minutes
Servings: 8
Preferred Wood Pellet: Oak or Alder

INGREDIENTS:

- 4 Chicken Breast (boneless/skinless)
- 2 ounce Grande Gringo Mexican Seasoning
- 12 ounce Bacon (crumbled)
- 4 ounce Monterey Jack Cheese
- 4 ounce Sharp Cheddar Cheese
- 1 cup Killer Hogs BBQ Sauce
- 2 to 3 Green Onions (chopped)

DIRECTIONS:

1. Prepare the smoker for cooking at 325.
2. Apply the Grande Gringo Mexican seasoning all over the chicken breast.
3. Placing the breasts on the smoker and inserting a test thermometer to check the internal temperature
4. Change the chicken breasts to a level iron skillet and cover with Killer Hogs BBQ Sauce when the internal temperature reaches
1. 155. Cook the breasts until the interior temperature reaches 165.
5. Add crumbled bacon, cheddar, and jack cheddar to the top of each breast. Cook for 3 to 5 minutes more, or until the cheese has melted on top.
6. Green onions should be added to the Monterey Chicken before serving.

NUTRITION: Calories: 420, Carbs: 43g, Fat: 15g, Protein: 26g

Smoke-Roasted Chicken Thighs

Preparation time: 1 hour
Cooking time: 2 hours
Servings: 4 to 6
Preferred Wood Pellet: Oak or Alder

INGREDIENTS:

- 3 pounds chicken thighs
- 2 teaspoons salt
- 2 teaspoons freshly ground black pepper
- 2 teaspoons garlic powder
- 2 teaspoons onion powder
- 2 cups prepared Italian dressing

DIRECTIONS:

1. Sprinkle the chicken with salt, pepper, garlic powder, and onion powder, being sure to get under the skin.
2. Cover with the Italian dressing, coating all sides, and refrigerate for 1 hour.
3. Cook the chicken and do not turn the thighs during the smoking process.

NUTRITION: Calories: 260, Carbs: 1g, Fat: 20g, Protein: 19g

Maple Smoked Sweet and Spicy Wings

Preparation time: 30 minutes
Cooking time: 1 1/2 hours
Servings: 8-10
Preferred Wood Pellet: Maple

INGREDIENTS:

- 5 lbs chicken wings
- 2 and 1/2 tbsp black pepper
- 1 tbsp onion powder
- 1 tbsp garlic salt
- 1 tbsp paprika Sauce
- 1 cup honey
- 1/2 cup hot BBQ sauce
- 3 tbsp apple juice

DIRECTIONS:

1. Mix the paprika, honey, onion powder, and garlic salt in a bowl.
2. Put the wings in a bag with the spice mix.
3. Shake, then let it rest for 30 minutes.
4. Place your preferred Wood Pellet Chips inside, then set the smoker temperature to 250 degrees F.
5. 30 minutes of smoking the meat on the top rack.
6. After that, switch and continue the smoking process for 25 more minutes.
7. Take out the meat when the internal smoke temperature reaches 160 degrees Fahrenheit.
8. Use a saucepan, combine the apple juice and honey BBQ sauce, and heat through.

9. Place the wings in a foil pan and drizzle the sauce over them.
10. Once again, smoke for a further 25 minutes in a smoker (second rack).
11. Serve and Enjoy!

NUTRITION: Calories 108, Fats 4g, Carbs 9g, Protein 7g

Herb Roasted Turkey

Preparation time: 15 Minutes
Cooking time: 3 Hours 30 Minutes
Servings: 12
Preferred Wood Pellet: Hickory

INGREDIENTS:

- 14 pounds turkey, cleaned
- 2 tablespoons chopped mixed herbs
- Pork and poultry rub as needed
- 1/4 teaspoon ground black pepper
- 3 tablespoons butter, unsalted, melted
- 8 tablespoons butter, unsalted, softened
- 2 cups chicken broth

DIRECTIONS:

1. The turkey should be cleaned by removing the giblets, washed from the inside out, dried with paper towels, and placed on a roasting pan, and its wings should be tucked with butcher's thread.
2. Turn on the grill by pressing the power button on the control panel, fill the grill hopper with hickory-flavored wood pellets, choosing "smoke" from the temperature dial, or setting the temperature to 325 °F and allowing it to heat for at least 15 minutes.
3. Meanwhile, make herb butter by placing melted butter in a small bowl, adding black pepper and mixed herbs, and beating until frothy.
4. Put some of the prepared herb butter beneath the turkey's skin and massage the skin to spread the butter evenly.

5. Add the liquid into the roasting pan, season with pork and poultry rub, and coat the outside of the turkey with the melted butter.
6. Open the grill lid after it has heated up, set the roasting pan with the turkey on the grill grate, close the grill, and smoke it for three hours and thirty minutes, until the top has gone golden brown.
7. When the turkey is finished, move it to a cutting board, let it rest for 30 minutes, then slice it and serve.

NUTRITION: Calories: 154.6; Fat: 3.1 g; Carbs: 8.4 g; Protein: 28.8 g

Turkey Legs

Preparation time: 10 Minutes
Cooking time: 5 Hours
Servings: 4
Preferred Wood Pellet: Hickory

INGREDIENTS:

- 4 turkey legs

For the Brine:

- 1/2 cup curing salt
- 1 tablespoon whole black peppercorns
- 1 cup BBQ rub
- 1/2 cup brown sugar
- 2 bay leaves
- 2 teaspoons liquid smoke
- 16 cups of warm water
- 4 cups ice
- 8 cups of cold water

DIRECTIONS:

1. To make the brine, fill a large stockpot with warm water, set it over high heat, add the peppercorns, bay leaves, and liquid smoke, toss in the salt, sugar, and BBQ rub, and then bring it to a boil.
2. Remove it from the heat and bring it to room temperature. Then add cold water and ice cubes, and let the brine cool in the refrigerator.
3. Then add the turkey legs, fully immerse them, and refrigerate for 24 hours to soak.
4. Remove the turkey legs from the brine after 24 hours, give them a good rinse, and then pat dry using paper towels.

5. Put on the grill by using the control panel, selecting "smoke" on the temperature dial, or setting the temperature to 250 degrees F and letting the grill warm for at least 15 minutes.
6. Open the lid once the grill is hot, add the turkey legs to the grill grate, close the grill, and smoke for five hours, or until the turkey is well browned and the internal temperature reaches 165 degrees Fahrenheit. Serve right away.

NUTRITION: Calories: 416; Fat: 13.3 g; Carbs: 0 g; Protein: 69.8g

Turkey Breast

Preparation time: 12 Hours
Cooking time: 8 Hours
Servings: 6
Preferred Wood Pellet: Apple-flavored wood

INGREDIENTS:

For The Brine:
- 2 pounds turkey breast, deboned
- 2 tablespoons ground black pepper
- 1/4 cup salt
- 1 cup brown sugar
- 4 cups cold water

For The BBQ Rub:
- 2 tablespoons dried onions
- 2 tablespoons garlic powder
- 1/4 cup paprika
- 2 tablespoons ground black pepper
- 1 tablespoon salt
- 2 tablespoons brown sugar
- 2 tablespoons red chili powder
- 1 tablespoon cayenne pepper
- 2 tablespoons sugar
- 2 tablespoons ground cumin

DIRECTIONS:

1. Take a sizable bowl, add sugar, salt, and black pepper to it, then add water and whisk until the sugar is dissolved to prepare the brine.
2. Put the turkey breast in it, fully immerse it, and refrigerate it for at least 12 hours to allow it to soak.

3. Prepare the BBQ rub in the meanwhile. To do this, take a small dish, add all ingredients, and whisk to combine. Set the bowl aside until needed.
4. Once the turkey breast has been removed from the brine, thoroughly season it with the prepared BBQ rub.
5. When you're ready to cook, turn on the grill, add apple-flavored wood pellets to the grill hopper, turn on the grill using the control panel, choose "smoke" on the temperature dial, and wait at least 15 minutes.
6. Open the grill's lid after it has heated up, add the turkey breast to the grill grate, close the grill, raise the smoking temperature to 225 degrees Fahrenheit, and smoke the turkey for 8 hours, or until the internal temperature reaches 160 degrees Fahrenheit.
7. When the turkey is finished cooking, move it to a cutting board, let it rest for 10 minutes, then slice it and serve.

NUTRITION: Calories: 250; Fat: 5 g; Carbs: 31 g; Protein: 18 g

Apple Wood-Smoked Whole Turkey

Preparation time: 10 minutes
Cooking time: 5 hours
Preferred Wood Pellet: Apple
Servings: 6

INGREDIENTS:

- 1 (10- to 12-pound) turkey, giblets removed
- Extra-virgin olive oil, for rubbing
- 1/4 cup poultry seasoning
- 8 tablespoons (1 stick) unsalted butter, melted
- 1/2 cup apple juice
- 2 teaspoons dried sage
- 2 teaspoons dried thyme

DIRECTIONS:

1. Supply your smoker with wood pellets.
2. Preheat with the lid closed to 250°F.
3. Rub the turkey with oil and then season with the poultry seasoning inside and out, getting under the skin.
4. Mix the melted butter, apple juice, sage, and thyme for basting.
5. Place the turkey in a pan, place it on the grill, close the lid, and grill for 5 to 6 hours.
6. Let the turkey meat rest for about 15 to 20 minutes before carving.

NUTRITION: Calories: 180; Carbs: 3g; Fat: 2g; Protein: 39g

BBQ Whole Turkey

Preparation time: 25 Minutes
Cooking time: 4 Hours & 30 Minutes
Servings: 6 Persons
Preferred Wood Pellet: Apricot or Alder

INGREDIENTS:

- Whole turkey – 2 pounds
- Turkey brine kit – 1
- Turkey rub – 1 cup
- Spicy BBQ sauce – 1 1/2 cup
- Butter, unsalted, softened – 1/2 cup

DIRECTIONS:

1. The turkey should be brined as directed on the package before the grill is heated.
2. The turkey should then be taken out of the brine, thoroughly rinsed, dried, and brought to room temperature.
3. To make the sauce, take a medium bowl and whisk together 1/2 cup of the BBQ sauce and the butter.
4. Ensure the skin is connected and intact before removing the skin off the turkey's legs and breasts with your hands. Next, put the prepared sauce below the skin in a uniform layer.
5. After that, massage the outside of the bird well with the turkey rub.
6. Place the whole turkey on the grilling rack after it has heated up and let it smoke for 30 minutes.
7. When the control panel indicates an interior temperature of 160 degrees F, raise the grill's temperature to 300 degrees F; continue cooking for an additional 4 hours.

8. After an hour of smoking, check the fire and add additional wood pallets if needed.
9. Brush the remaining BBQ sauce over the turkey and continue cooking it for an additional 20 minutes or until it is well coated.
10. After finishing cooking, take the turkey from the grill and allow it to rest for 25 minutes.
11. Then carve the turkey into slices and serve immediately.

NUTRITION: Calories: 94; Fat: 2g; Carbs: 1g; Protein: 18g

Lamb

Garlic Lamb Cutlets

Preparation time: 10-15 minutes
Cooking time: 3 hours
Servings: 4
Preferred Wood Pellet: Oak or Alder

INGREDIENTS:

- 6 garlic cloves
- 2 tablespoons apple cider vinegar
- 1/2 cup of water
- 1/4 cup extra virgin olive oil
- 1 teaspoon salt
- 1 teaspoon pepper
- 4 pounds lamb cutlets

DIRECTIONS:

1. Take a bowl and add minced garlic, vinegar, water, olive oil, salt, and pepper
2. Rub the mixture thoroughly over lamb cutlets and transfer them to your fridge; let them chill for 4 hours
3. Remove from fridge and let them sit for 45 minutes
4. Take your drip pan and add water; cover it with aluminum foil. Preheat your smoker to 225 degrees F
5. Use water to fill the water pan halfway through and place it over the drip pan. Add wood chips to the side tray
6. Place meat on the top rack and smoke for 3 hours or until the internal temperature reaches 150 degrees F
7. Remove chops and let them cool for 15 minutes
8. Serve and enjoy!

NUTRITION: Calories: 419, Fat: 28g, Carbohydrates: 0.82g, Protein: 36g

Smoked Lamb Shoulder

Preparation time: 15 minutes
Cooking time: 1 hr. 30 minutes
Servings: 4
Preferred Wood Pellet: Hard Wood Mesquite

INGREDIENTS:

- 5 lb. lamb shoulder, boneless and excess fat trimmed
- 2 Tbsp. kosher salt
- 2 Tbsp. black pepper
- Tbsp. rosemary, dried

The Injection
- 1 cup apple cider vinegar

The Spritz
- 1 cup apple cider vinegar
- 1 cup apple juice

DIRECTIONS:

1. Preheat the wood pellet smoker with a water pan to 2250°F.
2. Rinse the lamb in cold water and then dry it with a paper towel. Inject vinegar into the lamb.
3. Dry the lamb again and rub it with oil, salt, black pepper and rosemary. Tie with kitchen twine.
4. Smoke uncovered for 1 hour, then spritz every 15 minutes until the internal temperature reaches 190°F.
5. Take the lamb off the grill and then place it on a platter. Let it cool before shredding it and enjoying it with your favorite side.

NUTRITION: Calories: 240, Fat: 19g, Protein: 17g

Smoked Pulled Lamb Sliders

Preparation time: 10 minutes
Cooking time: 3 hours
Servings: 7
Preferred Wood Pellet: Hard Wood Mesquite

INGREDIENTS:

- 5 lb. lamb shoulder, boneless
- 1/2 cup olive oil
- 1/4 cup dry rub 10-ounce spritz

The Dry Rub
- 1/3 cup kosher salt
- 1/3 cup pepper, ground
- 1-1/3 cup garlic, granulated

The Spritz
- 4 ounce Worcestershire sauce
- 6-ounce apple cider vinegar

DIRECTIONS:

1. Preheat the wood pellet smoker with a water bath to 250°F.
2. Trim any fat from the lamb, then rub with oil and dry rub.
3. Place the lamb on the smoker for 90 minutes, then spritz with a spray bottle.
4. Transfer the lamb shoulder to a foil pan with the remaining spritz liquid and cover tightly with foil.
5. Place back in the smoker and smoke until the internal temperature reaches 200°F.
6. Let it rest, serving with slaw, bun, or aioli.
7. Enjoy!

NUTRITION: Calories: 339, Fat: 22g, Carbs: 16g, Protein: 18g

Crown Rack of Lamb

Preparation time: 10 minutes
Cooking time: 30 minutes
Servings: 6
Preferred Wood Pellet: Hard Wood Mesquite

INGREDIENTS:

- 2 racks of lamb, drenched
- Tbsp. garlic, crushed
- 1 Tbsp. rosemary, finely chopped
- 1/4 cup olive oil
- Twine

DIRECTIONS:

1. Rinse the racks with cold water and then dry them with a paper towel.
2. Lay the racks on a flat board, then score about 1/4 inch down between each bone.
3. Mix garlic, rosemary, and oil in a mixing bowl, then generously brush on the lamb.
4. Take each lamb rack and bend it into a semicircle forming a crown-like shape.
5. Use the twine to wrap the racks about 4 times, from the base to the top. Make sure you tie the twine tightly to keep the racks together.
6. Preheat the wood pellet to 400-450°F, then place the lamb racks on a baking dish.
7. Cook for 10 minutes, then reduces the temperature to 300°F. Cook for 20 minutes or till the internal temperature reaches 130°F.

8. Remove the lamb rack from the wood pellet and let rest for 15 minutes.
9. Serve when hot with veggies and potatoes.

NUTRITION: Calories: 390, Fat: 35g, Protein: 17g

Lamb's Leg Traditional Steaks

Preparation time: 10 minutes
Cooking time: 10 minutes
Servings: 4
Preferred Wood Pellet: Hard Wood Mesquite

INGREDIENTS:

- 4 lamb steaks, bone-in
- 1/4 cup olive oil
- 4 garlic cloves, minced
- Tbsp. rosemary, freshly chopped
- Salt and black pepper

DIRECTIONS:

1. Put the lamb in a shallow dish in a single layer and then top with oil, garlic cloves, rosemary, salt, and black pepper.
2. Let sit for 30 minutes.
3. Preheat the wood pellet grill and brush the grill grate with oil.
4. Place the lamb meats on the grill grate and cook until browned and the internals are slightly pink. The internal temperature should be 140°F.
5. Let rest for 5 minutes before serving.
6. Enjoy.

NUTRITION: Calories: 325, Fat: 22g, Carbs: 2g, Protein: 30g

Braised Lamb 'n Apricot

Preparation time: 15 minutes
Cooking time: 2 hours 30 minutes
Servings: 7
Preferred Wood Pellet: Hard Wood Mesquite

INGREDIENTS:

- Leg of a lamb of about 4 to 6 lbs. with the aitchbone removed
- Green Mountain Wild Game Rub
- Tbsp. of minced garlic

For the Apricot-Mustard Glaze:
- 1 Jar of about 10 Ounce of apricot jelly
- 1/4 Cup of yellow mustard
- 1 Tsp. of garlic powder

DIRECTIONS:

1. Start by rubbing the lamb generously with the Wild Game Rub and the minced garlic.
2. Grill at a temperature of about 400°F for about 30 minutes, turning at least once
3. While the lamb is being cooked, combine the glaze ingredients in a medium saucepan and let simmer for about 15 minutes.
4. Decrease the heat to about 325°F and cook for about 60 minutes.
5. Brush the lamb with the prepared glaze a few times during the last 30 minutes.
6. Remove the lamb meat from the wood pellet grill and cover with foil for about 10 minutes.
7. Serve and enjoy your dish!

NUTRITION: Calories: 250, Fat: 18g, Carbohydrates: 6g, Protein: 21g

Greek-Style Roast Leg of Lamb

Preparation time: 25 minutes
Cooking time: 1 hr. 35 minutes
Servings: 6
Preferred Wood Pellet: Hard Wood Mesquite

INGREDIENTS:

- 6 tablespoons extra-virgin olive oil
- Leg of lamb (6 to 7 pounds), bone-in
- Juice of 2 lemons, freshly squeezed
- 1 Sprig of fresh rosemary, stems discarded, stripped needles
- 1 sprig of fresh oregano
- 8 garlic cloves
- Freshly ground black pepper and kosher salt (coarse) as required

DIRECTIONS:

1. Use a sharp paring knife to cut a series of tiny slices into the meat. For garlic and herb paste:
2. Finely chop the oregano, garlic, and rosemary using a chef's knife and a clean, sizable chopping board. You may also put these items in a food processor.
3. Put a small amount of the prepared paste into each meat slit. Use any of the tools to put the paste into the slit.
4. Place the lamb coated on a rack within a large roasting pan.
5. Freshly squeezed lemon juice should be applied to the meat's exterior first, followed by olive oil. Cover with plastic wrap, then place in the fridge overnight.
6. The next day, take the meat out of the fridge and let it rest at room temperature for 30 minutes.

7. Remove the plastic wrap, then salt and pepper the meat to taste.
8. When ready, turn the wood pellet grill on the smoke setting and cook it for 4 to 5 minutes with the lid open. Set the smoker to 400 degrees Fahrenheit and shut the lid. The lamb needs to roast for 30 minutes.
9. Turn down the heat to 350°F and cook the lamb for an additional hour or until the internal temperature reaches 140°F.
10. Transfer the cooked lamb to a large, clean cutting board, let it rest for a few minutes; then cut it into thin slices against the grain. Serve hot and take pleasure in.

NUTRITION: Calories: 760, Fat: 64g, Cholesterol: 190mg, Carbs: 1g, Protein: 40g

Smoked Rack of Lamb

Preparation time: 20 minutes
Cooking time: 1 hour 20 minutes
Servings: 4
Preferred Wood Pellet: Hard Wood Mesquite

INGREDIENTS:

- A rack of lamb, preferably 4 to 5 pounds

For Marinade
- Medium lemon
- 4 garlic cloves, minced
- 1 teaspoon thyme
- 1/4 cup balsamic vinegar
- 1 teaspoon basil
- 1 teaspoon each of pepper and salt

For Glaze
- Tablespoons soy sauce
- 1/4 cup Dijon mustard
- Tablespoons Worcestershire sauce
- 1/4 cup dry red wine

DIRECTIONS:

1. The marinade ingredients should all be combined in a gallon-sized zip-lock bag.
2. After finishing, remove the silver skin from the lamb racks and place the trimmed racks in the marinade-filled gallon bag. Mix everything, then chill the bag overnight.
3. Preheat your wood pellet to 300°F. Meanwhile, combine all of the glaze's components in a large mixing basin.

4. Put the rack of lamb on the hot grill after the glaze has been combined and it has been prepared.
5. After 12 to 15 minutes of cooking, baste the racks with the prepared glaze mixture.
6. After flipping, cook the rack for about an hour or until it registers an internal temperature of between 135 and 145 °F. Remember to brush the meat with the glaze every 30 minutes.
7. When done, take the meat from the grill and set it aside to rest for a few minutes.
8. As desired, cut the meat into pieces; serve hot; and enjoy.

NUTRITION: Calories: 780, Fat: 60g, Cholesterol: 200mg, Carbs: 5g, Protein: 50g

Smoked Lamb Loin

Preparation time: 20 minutes
Cooking time: 50 minutes
Servings: 6
Preferred Wood Pellet: Apple and Pecan

INGREDIENTS:

- 10 to 12 Lamb loin chops
- Jeff's Original rub recipe
- Rosemary, finely chopped
- Olive oil
- Coarse kosher salt

DIRECTIONS:

1. Put the chops on a cooling rack or cookie sheet.
2. Sprinkle salt liberally over the top of the chops before dry brining.
3. Once finished, take the covered meat out of the fridge, being careful not to rinse it.
4. Pour around 1/4 cup of olive oil over 1 tablespoon of chopped rosemary to make an infusion of olive oil and rosemary. After setting the mixture away, let it an hour to settle.
5. Your lamb chops should be topped and sides with the prepared mixture.
6. Sprinkle the rub on the chops' top, sides, and bottom.
7. Set your smoker to indirect heat at 225 degrees.
8. Make careful you smoke using a combination of apple and pecan for the best results.

9. Cook the coated chops for 40 to 50 minutes or until they register 138°F inside.
10. Enjoy a hot serving.

NUTRITION: Calories: 650, Fat: 50g, Cholesterol: 155mg, Carbs: 1g, Protein: 42g

Seasoned Lamb Shoulder

Preparation time: 15 minutes
Cooking time: 5 hours 45 minutes
Servings: 6
Preferred Wood Pellet: Hard Wood Apple

INGREDIENTS:

- 1 (5-pound) bone-in lamb shoulder, trimmed
- 3-4 tablespoons Moroccan seasoning
- 2 tablespoons olive oil
- 1 cup water
- 1/4 cup apple cider vinegar

DIRECTIONS:

1. Preheat the Wood Pellet Grill & Smoker on the smoke setting to 275 degrees F.
2. Coat the lamb shoulder with oil evenly, then rub it with Moroccan seasoning.
3. Put the lamb shoulder on the grill and cook for about 45 minutes.
4. In a food-safe spray bottle, mix vinegar and water.
5. Spray the lamb shoulder with the vinegar mixture evenly.
6. Cook for about 4-5 hours, spraying with vinegar mixture every 20 minutes.
7. Remove the lamb shoulder from the grill and place it onto a cutting board for about 20 minutes before slicing.
8. Cut the lamb into desired-sized slices and serve.

NUTRITION: Calories 563, Total Fat 25.2 g, Saturated Fat 7.5 g, Cholesterol 251 mg, Sodium 1192 mg, Total Carbs 3.1 g, Fiber 0 g, Sugar 1.4 g, Protein 77.4 g

Conclusion

Throughout this guide, we have seen how a pellet grill works and numerous tips on cooking, cutting and cleaning methods. In addition, you have learned about hundreds of delicious recipes.

I hope you have discovered new things about the world of barbecue and have enjoyed the tips and tactics scattered throughout the book.

www.ingramcontent.com/pod-product-compliance
Lightning Source LLC
Chambersburg PA
CBHW050248120526
44590CB00016B/2266